I0041969

Children with Emotional
and Behavioral Disorders

Children with Emotional and Behavioral Disorders

Systemic Practice

Marianne Celano

MP MOMENTUM PRESS
HEALTH

MOMENTUM PRESS, LLC, NEW YORK

Children with Emotional and Behavioral Disorders: Systemic Practice

Copyright © Momentum Press, LLC, 2018.

All rights reserved. No part of this publication may be reproduced, stored in a retrieval system, or transmitted in any form or by any means—electronic, mechanical, photocopy, recording, or any other except for brief quotations, not to exceed 400 words, without the prior permission of the publisher.

First published in 2018 by
Momentum Press, LLC
222 East 46th Street, New York, NY 10017
www.momentumpress.net

ISBN-13: 978-1-94561-298-5 (paperback)
ISBN-13: 978-1-94561-299-2 (e-book)

Momentum Press Psychology Collection

Cover and interior design by Exeter Premedia Services Private Ltd., Chennai, India

First edition: 2018

10 9 8 7 6 5 4 3 2 1

Printed in the United States of America.

Abstract

This concise book is for students and therapists who wish to develop competencies in family therapy and systemic practice with children. Using a fictional clinical case, the book describes the contributions of Couple and Family Psychology (CFP) to the understanding and treatment of emotional and behavioral disorders among children ages 2 to 12. CFP competencies are presented and applied to the case of a 9 year old girl with school refusal and behavior problems. The book describes how a systemic perspective affects clinical decisions from intake to treatment termination. Specific competencies discussed include: scientific knowledge, assessment, evidence-based practice, intervention, individual and cultural diversity, ethical and legal standards, and reflective practice. Readers will come away from this book with a clear sense of how to conceptualize and treat common childhood emotional and behavioral disorders from a systemic perspective.

Keywords

child treatment, children, competencies, couple and family psychology, emotional and behavioral problems, family intervention, family therapy, systemic practice

Contents

Chapter 1   Introduction to Family Psychology: The Medina Family 1

Chapter 2   The Science Supporting a Family Systems Approach.......13

Chapter 3   Family Assessment and Systemic Case Conceptualization...29

Chapter 4   Evidence-Based Practice and Treatment Planning 45

Chapter 5   Systemic Interventions.....................................65

Chapter 6   Foundational Competencies and Termination.................85

About the Author...99

Index 101

CHAPTER 1

Introduction to Family Psychology: The Medina Family

Learning how to do psychotherapy with children and their families is a complex process that takes time, supervised experience, and mastery of a broad base of knowledge, skills, and attitudes. The application of a systemic perspective to this work adds even more complexity, but also yields greater returns, as it addresses the multiple contexts in which children's development is embedded. What is a systemic perspective, and how does it affect clinical decisions at a family's entry into services? These questions are best answered in part through case illustration. The following sections introduce a family that is the focus of this book, describe how a systemic perspective guides early clinical decisions, and discusses the goals of the book.

A Family in Crisis

Emilio and Karen Medina were referred to the clinic by their pediatrician, Dr. Shin, for evaluation of their nine-year-old daughter, Elena. Presenting problems include irritability, stomach aches, difficulty sleeping, nightmares, poor concentration, impulsivity, tantrums, and refusal to attend school consistently. The parents report that Elena has always been a "difficult child," but her tantrums have grown more severe and frequent over the last year, and in recent weeks, she has refused to go to school three to four days per week, complaining of stomach aches. Dr. Shin has evaluated and treated Elena's stomach pain, and will not provide any more medical excuses for her absences.

The Medina family consists of Emilio, age 45; Karen, age 39; Elena, age nine; and Julian, age six. Emilio is a software engineer who works full time;

Karen is a nurse who works part time. Julian (1st grade) and Elena (4th grade) attend the same public elementary school. The family lives in a suburb of Atlanta.

This is the information available on an intake form in an outpatient clinic. In many behavioral health (BH) organizations, the referred child and a parent will participate in a diagnostic evaluation or intake session before treatment decisions and recommendations are made. However, BH providers often make case assignments based on only limited information, such as the preceding brief case description. For example, should the case be assigned to a clinician who does individual child therapy or family therapy? Should it be given to a trainee or a seasoned BH clinician (henceforth called "clinician")? If the organization has specialty clinics, should the family be evaluated in the anxiety disorders clinic or the behavior disorders clinic?

The Role of Theory in Clinical Decisions

It is at this early juncture that the practitioner's theoretical orientation influences clinical decision-making. For a clinician assigned Elena Medina, theory guides which questions are asked, how the presenting problem is explained, and which interventions are recommended. A clinician with strong grounding in attachment theory would inquire about Elena's earliest years of life, the history and quality of her relationships with her primary caregivers, and any threats to the stability and continuity of these relationships. A clinician with a cognitive behavioral theoretical orientation would explore the antecedents and contingencies for Elena's symptoms and challenging behaviors, and ultimately recommend individual cognitive behavioral therapy (CBT). A clinician well-versed in psychodynamic approaches might recommend play therapy.

By contrast, a clinician with a family systems orientation conceptualizes the problems of children as embedded within a matrix of reciprocal interaction between intrapersonal, interpersonal, and environmental factors. A systems framework is not inconsistent with attachment-based, cognitive behavioral, or psychodynamic formulations of disordered child behavior. A systems perspective may be inclusive of some or all of these formulations, but embeds them within a larger framework that includes the relationships within the family (nuclear and extended), and the child's and family's relationships in the community (e.g., parents' employer and friends, child's peers and school, religious organizations, systems of care). Application of a family systems orientation to clinical work does not necessarily result in a recommendation for family therapy.

Application of a Systemic Perspective to the Case

Application of a systemic paradigm to the Medina case generates a number of questions:

1. How do the parents understand Elena's problems? How do others in the family understand it? Do the parents view the problem similarly or differently?
2. From whom do the parents obtain emotional and instrumental support in childrearing?
3. From which doctors, school personnel, and others in the community have the parents sought help for Elena's problems? How do family members describe their help-seeking experience?
4. How do Elena's problems affect her parents, their relationship with one another and with Elena, and the parents' relationships with others?
5. How do Elena's problems affect her younger brother, her relationship with him, or her parents' relationship with him?
6. What is the function, if any, of Elena's behavior problems?

The clinician can ask the parent(s) one or more of these questions in a telephone conversation prior to making a decision about case assignment or a recommendation about who should attend the first assessment session. One advantage of asking these questions is that they allow the parents to share their thoughts and concerns, to receive validation and support, and to begin to develop a measure of trust in the clinician. A second advantage is that these questions communicate an expectation of collaboration between clinician and family in solving the presenting problems. Third, parents who have explored these questions are likely to bring to the assessment session family members in addition to the referred child, if they are invited to do so. Finally, the clinician obtains important information to guide assessment decisions.

For the Medina family, these questions yielded the following information, obtained by the intake clinician during a 20-minute phone call with the mother:

Karen believes that Elena tries to be perfect, and is too competitive in school and sports. She thinks her daughter is refusing school because she has recently experienced some verbal bullying from other 4th grade girls. Karen is frustrated with how clingy and demanding her daughter has become, and she worries that Julian, a comparatively easy and cheerful child, will start acting like his sister. She reports that Emilio is "harder" on Elena than she is, but also loses his temper with her more easily. He reportedly views Elena's behavior as manipulative and attention-seeking, and the parents often disagree about the best way to discipline her.

The parents are too embarrassed to discuss Elena's behavior problems with their friends. There are no extended family members in Atlanta. Emilio's parents and sisters live in south Florida; Karen's family members are more dispersed and live in the Northeast and the Midwest. Emilio is reportedly close with his parents and talks with his mother often. The paternal grandmother is also concerned about Elena's behavior, and has offered several suggestions, none of which has worked. Karen does not talk with her parents or siblings about Elena's behavior problems.

Karen and Emilio have discussed Elena's behavior problems with her teacher and school counselor. Both report that Elena is an excellent student and gets along well with peers. They have expressed concern about how many days Elena has missed school and have suggested that the parents consider a home-bound academic program if she cannot attend school regularly. Karen asked the pediatrician, Dr. Shin, to sign the form for home-bound instruction, but the doctor declined, referring the family to BH services for Elena instead.

The role of the clinician from this point forward will depend on the referral question, the developing hypotheses about the case, and the clinician's responsibilities in the BH clinic. Depending on the setting and the clinician's competencies, these responsibilities may include BH screening, consultation, referral, diagnostic evaluation, psychological testing, medication evaluation, and psychotherapy (individual, group or multigroup, couples, family). The referral questions for the Medina family may include: (a) to what extent do Elena's presenting problems reflect psychiatric problems that can be addressed by BH services?, (b) what is Elena's psychiatric diagnosis?, (c) to what extent are family and community processes contributing to Elena's presenting problems?, and (d) what BH intervention(s) are recommended?

A Family Psychology Framework for Child Problems

Child Behavioral and Emotional Problems

Emotional and behavioral disorders are common among children. Approximately 13 to 20 percent of the children in the United States experience these disorders (Perou et al., 2013); globally, one in four children and adolescents experience a psychiatric disorder in a given year (Merikangas, Nakamura, & Kessler, 2009). In the United States, the rates of clinically significant behavioral and emotional difficulties are even higher for children from economically disadvantaged families (Webster-Stratton & Hammond, 1998) and higher still (50 percent) for children in foster care (Burns et al., 2004). The most commonly diagnosed childhood psychiatric disorder is attention-deficit/hyperactivity disorder (ADHD), affecting 8.5 percent of the children 8 to 15 years old (Merikangas et al., 2009). Anxiety disorders also are prevalent, occurring in 6 to 9 percent of children under age 13 (Beesdo, Knappe, & Pine, 2009). In addition, disruptive behavior disorders are common; the prevalence of oppositional defiant disorder (ODD) is approximately 3.3 percent (American Psychiatric Association, 2013). However, prevalence estimates of psychiatric disorders underestimate the number of children with significant clinical impairments (Brotman et al., 2006).

Couple and Family Psychology

Family psychology, or couple and family psychology (CFP) as it is known by the American Board of Professional Psychology (ABPP), is a specialty in professional psychology that utilizes a systemic epistemology to assess and treat issues of psychological health and pathology among individuals, couples, families, and larger social systems. CFP specialists conceptualize behavior within a theoretical framework that recognizes the reciprocal interaction among individual (biological and psychological variables), interpersonal, and contextual factors over time. Children's emotional and behavioral problems are seen as embedded within transactional processes occurring within and across the levels of the individual child, the family, and other environmental contexts, including the school, peer group, health-care teams, and systems of care. Individual factors (e.g., identities, beliefs) and interpersonal interaction patterns are nested within and influenced by broader contextual variables (e.g., culture, age, religion), and one or more of these variables (e.g., gender) may influence others (e.g., race).

This systemic epistemology is often different from theories about psychopathology typically taught in psychology and psychiatry training settings. For example, psychologists and psychiatrists usually learn how to apply a biopsychosocial case formulation, which requires identification and integration of etiological influences from biological, psychological, and social domains. A biopsychosocial formulation of the Medina case would consider the potential causal mechanisms of Elena's difficulties with executive functioning (e.g., impulsivity, poor concentration) and physiological reactivity, her negative thoughts about school, the perceived bullying from peers, and the parents' inconsistent (and incompatible) reactions to her difficult behavior.

A systemic case conceptualization is more than a biopsychosocial formulation. A CFP specialist would consider the same biopsychosocial etiological factors, but would also attend to: (a) how they interact with one another over time, and (b) the historical and sociocultural context of childrearing for the family. A systemic formulation would explore not just the impact on Elena of the parents' disagreements regarding discipline, but also the impact of Elena's symptoms and negative behavior on the parents' individual functioning, parent-child relationship, and marital relationship, which in turn may contribute to the severity, frequency, or duration of the presenting problems. In addition, the CFP specialist would explore how broader sociocultural factors (e.g., cultural values related to childrearing) and historical factors (e.g., parents' experiences in their families of origin) contribute to more proximal etiological factors, such as parenting behavior and the conflicting parental reactions to Elena's challenging behavior.

CFP Approach to Treatment of Children

A CFP approach to treatment of children's emotional and behavioral disorders can be justified on theoretical, empirical, and ethical grounds. The potential impact of the environment on child psychopathology has been recognized since 1920, when John B. Watson used classical conditioning to create fear in a young child (Watson & Rayner, 1920). Current developmental models of children's emotional and behavioral problems are strongly influenced by: (a) ecological theories of human development (Bronfenbrenner, 1986), which posit that child behavior is the result of individual characteristics (e.g., irritable temperament) as well as the progressively broader social contexts within which child development is embedded; and (b) transactional theories of development, which describe how child behaviors and environmental factors influence one another over time to yield BH outcomes (Sameroff, 2009). Like developmental models of child psychopathology, family systems theories articulate important links between family processes and children's emotional and behavioral problems. For example, the structural family theory explains presenting problems in terms of maladaptive family boundaries or interaction patterns, whereas a strategic or systemic approach states that symptoms are maintained by the family's unsuccessful problem-solving attempts.

Empirical research has established the etiological role of family and parenting processes in the development of child behavior disorders. For example, parental depression and couple conflict contribute to inconsistent and harsh parenting, which in turn lead to children's aggressive behavior (Barry, Dunlap, Lochman, & Wells, 2009). Not surprisingly, family interventions have demonstrated efficacy and effectiveness in treating children's emotional and behavioral disorders. In fact, systemic interventions are the treatment of choice for child behavior problems, including ODD and conduct disorder (Baldwin, Christian, Berkeljon, & Shadish, 2012). Family therapy is an important adjunctive treatment for ADHD, anxiety, autism, depression, and eating disorders in children and adolescents (Kaslow et al., 2012).

There are also ethical arguments for a CFP approach to treatment of emotional and behavioral disorders in children. First, BH service delivery for children increasingly is guided by a *systems of care* approach, in which multiple agencies work collaboratively with the family to provide and coordinate services, or by an interdisciplinary health-care team. CFP provides the knowledge, skills, and attitudes to understand and intervene respectfully in the complex and complementary processes characterizing interactions between systems (e.g., school and family) and within the health-care team. Second, a systemic perspective is foundational to multiculturalism and cultural competence (Harway et al., 2012). Because a systemic epistemology focuses on the relationships in a particular system within a broader sociocultural context, a CFP specialist is not likely to propose an intervention that violates a family's belief system or culturally influenced relationship patterns. In summary, a CFP approach to treatment of children's behavioral and emotional disorders is warranted given the demonstrated contribution of family psychology science and practice to children's behavioral health care, the need for clinicians to work with multiple health-care disciplines or systems of care, and the professional mandate of cultural competence in clinical work with all populations.

The arguments for using a systemic framework to treat childhood emotional and behavioral problems are so convincing and longstanding that it is hard to imagine a child clinical practice not guided by a systemic model. Indeed, virtually all of the professional disciplines engaged in BH services recommend a family assessment as part of an evaluation of child psychopathology. For example, according to the American Academy of Child and Adolescent Psychiatry (Josephson, 2007), a family assessment that includes observation of family interaction is always indicated in the psychiatric evaluation of a child. Similarly, social workers are trained to conduct a comprehensive assessment of the family system to determine the needs of the child, particularly in child welfare systems. Consideration of individuals in context has become part of the status quo in health service psychology.

These observations attest to the penetration of family systems theories and the successful dissemination of systemic practice. However, many clinicians who apply a systemic model do so inconsistently or in a piecemeal fashion. They may apply a systemic model to assessment, but not to intervention, or they may utilize systemic concepts, but not specialty knowledge derived from research. For example, a clinician evaluating the Medina family may fail to consider research on family processes associated with child anxiety, or evidence-based family interventions for behavior problems.

It is the integration of systemic science and practice that distinguishes family psychology from family therapy. Family therapy is a treatment modality that is usually guided by a systemic perspective. Family psychology is a specialty area of health service psychology characterized by a distinctive configuration of systemic theories, models, and evidence-based practices for specified problems and populations. CFP offers a conceptual lens that affects all aspects of professional practice and research. CFP specialists treating child emotional and behavioral problems apply a systemic perspective to assessment, intervention, research, ethics, consideration of culture, and consultation with professionals within and across systems of care.

Goals of the Book

This book will focus on the application of CFP to the understanding and treatment of emotional and behavioral disorders among children aged 2 to 12. It will summarize scientific knowledge about family processes contributing to the development and maintenance of common child behavior problems (i.e., oppositional behavior and school refusal), as well as childhood anxiety. CFP research and its implications for assessment and intervention will be presented with the aim of guiding clinical decisions.

Competencies in CFP provide the organizing framework for the book. The CFP competencies describe advanced scientific and theoretical knowledge in the specialty and application of this knowledge to specialty practice. These competencies have been explained comprehensively by Stanton and Welsh (2011) and updated for health service psychologists (Celano, in press). For psychologists providing health services, foundational competencies include those related to professionalism, relationships, and science; functional competencies have been identified in the domains of application, education, and systems (Hatcher, 2013). Table 1.1 shows the essential components for the CFP competencies within the application domain. Although these competencies were developed for psychologists wishing to specialize in CFP, many are relevant to

Table 1.1 Competency benchmarks for couple and family Psychology: Application domain

Competency	Essential components
Evidence-based practice (EBP)	• Be knowledgeable of CFP evidence-based practice (EBP) and specialty interventions • Applies EBP in CFP to issues and populations • Values the role of research in intervention
Assessment	• Understands the nature and scope of CFP assessment methods, and the psychometrics of CFP assessment instruments • Applies assessment methods, competently using multiple methods of assessment appropriate to CFP and applying them to case conceptualization • Understands case conceptualization in the context of CFP service delivery, including a model for producing a systemic case conceptualization • Demonstrates a client-centered perspective in the case conceptualization and assessment processes • Produces a systemic case conceptualization, including a client-centered problem formulation, case formulation, and treatment formulation
Intervention	• Knows a broad range of CFP interventions • Selects, implements, and evaluates CFP interventions, including EBP interventions • Knows about the effectiveness of psychoeducation, specialty curriculum for psychoeducation, and the distinction between psychoeducation and psychotherapy • Provides CFP interventions designed to improve relationship health in individual, group, and community settings • Understands data regarding the effectiveness and cost of CFP interventions for a particular clinical context • Understands the common medical, dental, and health treatments for the targeted population as part of the medical or clinical context for CFP specialty practice
Consultation	• Be knowledgeable about consultation theory, research findings, roles, assessment, and methodology • Conduct effective CFP consultations, including a systemic needs assessment yielding a report and recommendations, and effective interventions as appropriate • Values ethical standards and respects individual and cultural diversity in consultation practice

Note: From Celano (in press).

the clinical work of those from other professional disciplines, including psychiatrists, clinical social workers, and professional counselors.

The aims of the book are to: (a) describe specific CFP competencies for working with children, including foundational scientific knowledge, ethics, and diversity competencies, as well as functional competencies related to assessment and treatment; and (b) demonstrate the application of these competencies to the evaluation and treatment of a nine-year-old child presenting with school refusal and behavior problems.

To facilitate an understanding of the Medina case that is grounded in CFP science, Chapter 2 summarizes empirical knowledge about the biological, psychological, family, and community processes linked to childhood anxiety and behavior problems. The chapter also discusses cultural and contextual factors that may influence children's presenting problems, help-seeking patterns, and involvement in systems of care. Chapter 3 demonstrates how to apply CFP assessment and case formulation competencies to the case, and Chapter 4 describes a number of evidence-based interventions for the identified problems, organizing them within a systemic and integrative framework. Chapter 5 describes the essential components of the CFP intervention competency in clinical work with children, applying them to the Medina family, and discusses how to collaborate with systems of care and monitor treatment progress. Chapter 6 draws on foundational competencies in CFP to present cultural and ethical considerations in working with the Medina family and discusses issues associated with termination of systemic treatment.

References

American Psychiatric Association. (2013). *Diagnostic and statistical manual of mental disorders (DSM-5®)*. American Psychiatric Pub.

Baldwin, S. A., Christian, S., Berkeljon, A., & Shadish, W. R. (2012). The effects of family therapies for adolescent delinquency and substance abuse: A meta-analysis. *Journal of Marital and Family Therapy, 38*(1), 281–304.

Barry, T. D., Dunlap, S. T., Lochman, J. E., & Wells, K. C. (2009). Inconsistent discipline as a mediator between maternal distress and aggression in boys. *Child & Family Behavior Therapy, 31*(1), 1–19.

Bronfenbrenner, U. (1986). Ecology of the family as a context for human development: Research perspectives. *Developmental Psychology, 22*(6), 723–742.

Brotman, M. A., Schmajuk, M., Rich, B. A., Dickstein, D. P., Guyer, A. E., Costello, E. J., Egger, H. L., Angold, A., Pine, D. S., & Leibenluft, E. (2006). Prevalence, clinical correlates, and longitudinal course of severe mood dysregulation in children. *Biological Psychiatry, 60*(9), 991–997.

Burns, B. J., Phillips, S. D., Wagner, H. R., Barth, R. P., Kolko, D. J., Campbell, Y., & Landsverk, J. (2004). Mental health need and access to mental health services by youths involved with child welfare: A national survey. *Journal of the American Academy of Child & Adolescent Psychiatry, 43*(8), 960–970.

Celano, M. P. (In press). Competencies in couple and family psychology for health service psychologists. In B. H. Fiese (Ed.-in-Chief), M. Celano, K. Deater-Deckard, E.N. Jouriles, & M. M. Whisman (Assoc. Eds.). *APA Handbook of Contemporary Family Psychology* (Vol. 3). Washington, DC: American Psychological Association.

Harway, M., Kadin, S., Gottlieb, M. C., Nutt, R. L., & Celano, M. (2012). Family psychology and systemic approaches: Working effectively in a variety of contexts. *Professional Psychology: Research and Practice, 43*(4), 315–327.

Hatcher, R. L., Fouad, N. A., Grus, C. L., Campbell, L. F., McCutcheon, S. R., & Leahy, K. L. (2013). Competency benchmarks: Practical steps toward a culture of competence. *Training and Education in Professional Psychology, 7*(2), 84–91.

Josephson, A. M., & AACAP Work Group on Quality Issues. (2007). Practice parameter for the assessment of the family. *Journal of the American Academy of Child & Adolescent Psychiatry, 46*(7), 922–937.

Kaslow, N. J., Broth, M. R., Smith, C. O., & Collins, M. H. (2012). Family-based interventions for child and adolescent disorders. *Journal of Marital and Family Therapy, 38*(1), 82–100.

Merikangas, K. R., Nakamura, E. F., & Kessler, R. C. (2009). Epidemiology of mental disorders in children and adolescents. *Dialogues in Clinical Neuroscience, 11*(1), 7–20.

Perou, R., Bitsko, R. H., Blumberg, S. J., Pastor, P., Ghandour, R. M., Gfroerer, J. C., Hedden, S. L., & et al. (2013). Mental health surveillance among children—United States, 2005–2011. *MMWR Surveill Summ 62* (Suppl 2), 1–35.

Sameroff, A. (2009). *The transactional model of development: How children and contexts shape each other*. Washington, DC: American Psychological Association.

Stanton, M., & Welsh, R. K. (2011). *Specialty competencies in couple and family psychology*. Oxford, UK: Oxford University Press.

Watson, J. B., & Rayner, R. (1920). Conditioned emotional reactions. *Journal of Experimental Psychology, 3*(1), 1–14.

Webster-Stratton, C., & Hammond, M. (1998). Conduct problems and level of social competence in head start children: Prevalence, pervasiveness, and associated risk factors. *Clinical Child and Family Psychology Review, 1*(2), 101–124.

CHAPTER 2

The Science Supporting a Family Systems Approach

To assess a child's presenting problems, it is best to use a guide that suggests which potential etiological mechanisms to explore. For Couple and Family Psychology (CFP), the guide is drawn from accumulated and integrated knowledge about child and family development, family functioning, and child psychopathology. This knowledge is derived primarily from scientific research, often based on theory. Areas of scientific and scholarly inquiry most relevant to the Medina case include child behavior problems, the relationship between family functioning and child psychopathology, and broader contextual influences on child psychopathology, help-seeking, and systems of care.

Child Behavior Problems

The term *behavior problems* can be broadly defined as actions of children that others find objectionable or inappropriate for the context. Embedded in this definition are two important distinctions: (a) the behaviors in question are objectionable to others, not necessarily to the child and (b) whether the behavior is inappropriate or objectionable depends on the context in which it is displayed. *Context* encompasses developmental, family, social, and cultural perspectives; for example, a pattern of temper tantrums by a seven-year old is more likely to be identified as a problem than the same behavior shown by a two-year old. Given that children's behavior problems are identified as objectionable by others, involvement of caregivers and teachers is essential in determining whether the problem lies primarily with the child, the context provided by caregivers and teachers, or in the fit between the child and the context.

Almost all child behavior problems are multi-determined, and few are pathognomonic of a particular symptom or psychiatric disorder. For example, aggressive behavior can reflect impulsivity, anger, or anxiety. Social withdrawal may be due to a number of factors, including depression, anxiety, and delayed social skills. Behavior problems are classified primarily by diagnostic categories in research, and in some training settings, with disruptive behavior (i.e., externalizing) problems considered separately from behavior problems due to depression or anxiety (i.e., internalizing problems). However, in clinical situations, as with the Medina family, both types of problems co-occur. Research on the underlying features of psychiatric disorders document a fair amount of comorbidity, suggesting that a transdiagnostic approach is most useful in etiological models of child psychopathology. The transdiagnostic approach focuses on the common underlying mechanisms for multiple disorders, such as coping styles, cognitive biases, and peer relations (Ehrenreich-May & Chu, 2014).

Family Functioning and Child Psychopathology

Psychopathology in children under 12 years has been linked with a host of nested individual (biological, psychological), family, social, and macrosystemic etiological factors, as well as with interactions among these factors over time.

Biological and Psychological Child Factors

Elena Medina's disruptive behaviors consist of irritability, poor concentration, impulsivity, oppositional behavior, and tantrums. Biological and psychological causal factors to consider include: (a) difficulties with executive functioning (impulsivity, organization, and attention); (b) *difficult* temperament or deficits in emotion regulation; (c) delayed or uneven development across cognitive, physical, emotional and social domains; and (d) negative attribution bias about self and others. Biological and psychological factors are not mutually exclusive and often are related to one another. For example, a delay in social and emotional development contributes to affective dysregulation and negative attributions of others' behavior. Problems with executive functioning or emotion regulation can lead to negative interactions with parents and peers, which may result in the child's perception of others as rejecting, with implications for future interpersonal interactions. Indeed, it is difficult to consider biological and psychological etiological factors outside of the social context in which they are embedded.

Difficult Temperament

When parents report that their child has always been *difficult* or *high maintenance*, clinicians should inquire about the child's perceived temperament, emotion regulation, and executive functioning. These factors may be heritable, or they may arise as a result of early experiences, such as childhood trauma (De Bellis & Zisk, 2014) or prenatal exposure to alcohol. It is now well established that early experiences, including those in utero, shape brain structure and function, which in turn affect children's behavior. A child temperament with a strong genetic basis is behavioral inhibition, which is characterized by increased physiological arousal and fear of novel stimuli (Kagan et al., 1984). Behavioral inhibition has been found to predict anxiety symptoms and anxiety disorders in children. A difficult or inhibited temperament may render children more vulnerable to negative parenting (Slagt et al., 2016) or to changes in parental behavior related to depression or other psychopathology.

Child Effects on Parent and Family Processes

Child behavior, influenced by biological factors (genetics, brain structure, and function), may evoke dysfunctional family interactions that maintain or escalate the problematic behavior. In the case of the Medina family, Elena's oppositional and impulsive behaviors may cause her parents to respond with expressed anger and unpredictable threats of harsh punishment, which may lead Elena to *dig in* or escalate her negative behavior, consistent with the coercion model described by Patterson (Patterson, 1976). Parent–child conflict is a consistently robust predictor of child psychopathology, playing a prominent role in etiological models of aggression and delinquency, even in children as young as five years (Eddy, Leve, & Fagot, 2001). As aversive family conflict both models and reinforces aggressive behavior, coercive cycles in parent–child relationships over time can result in continued aggression, rejection by prosocial peers, and involvement with deviant peers in later childhood.

Alternatively, the parents may *cave* to Elena's demands and refusals, or provide intermittent negative consequences for her disruptive behavior. These parental reactions may reinforce the challenging behavior, as well as teach Elena to relentlessly persist in refusals or demands, as her parents will eventually give in. A wealth of behavioral theory and research documents the role of inconsistent discipline in reinforcing disruptive child behavior.

Theory and research support evocative child effects on parenting behavior for different kinds of child psychopathology. For example, poor child self-control (i.e., deficits in sustained attention, persistence, and emotion regulation) has a bidirectional effect on harsh parenting in childhood, even when controlling for shared genetic risk (Cecil et al., 2012). Child genetic effects influence internalizing behaviors, which in turn contribute to maternal emotional overinvolvement (Narusyte et al., 2008). Similarly, high levels of child anxiety elicit maternal intrusiveness, which then serves to maintain or exacerbate the anxiety (Eley et al., 2010).

Family Causal Factors

Longitudinal studies suggest that family processes can lead to child behavior problems even in the absence of predisposing child biological or psychological factors. Family processes may contribute to the etiology of child psychopathology, or influence the course and severity of a disorder once it develops. Alternatively, poor family functioning and child psychopathology may be associated with one another because they share common roots, such as genetic characteristics, or because they are different manifestations of the same process, such as trauma exposure or social stress. Family factors most relevant to the Medina case include parenting, couple conflict, parental depression, and system-wide family dynamics.

Parenting

A large body of theory and research has established the significant role for parenting in the development of child psychopathology. The results from independent meta-analyses suggest that specific parenting practices are associated with childhood externalizing behavior problems, depression, and anxiety. For example, inconsistent or harsh discipline is linked to disruptive and oppositional child behavior (Rothbaum & Weisz, 1994). Parental rejection has been implicated in the development of childhood depression (McLeod, Weisz, & Wood, 2007), and parental control (over-involvement, excessive restrictiveness, and lower levels of autonomy granting) contributes to childhood anxiety (McLeod, Wood, & Weisz, 2007).

Parenting can also influence the course and severity of child psychiatric disorders. For children with anxiety disorders, parental overprotection and limited autonomy granting may increase anxiety by restricting children's opportunities to experience challenging situations and develop mastery and confidence in their coping abilities. In the case of Attention Deficit Hyperactivity Disorder (ADHD), parents' realistic expectations for children's behavior and consistent positive reinforcement of their sustained attention to tasks can reduce impairment related to attention deficits and impulsivity.

Parents often have difficulty understanding why the same parenting practices affect two or more siblings differently. Although suboptimal parenting is associated with negative child outcomes, children are differentially susceptible to environmental influences. In addition, the adverse effects of poor parenting can be buffered or amplified by other contextual factors. For example, genetic factors may moderate the effects of parenting on young children's adjustment: toddlers at genetic risk for psychopathology have been found to benefit from more structured parenting, whereas toddlers at low genetic risk benefitted from less-structured parenting (Leve et al., 2009). Neighborhoods perceived by families as high in involvement and cohesion attenuate the link between hostile parenting and child externalizing problems (Silk et al., 2004).

Even when parenting is not harsh or overinvolved, it may contribute to child behavior problems if it does not fit the child's needs or context, or if one parent's method of discipline conflicts with that of the other parent. As parents generally adopt the parenting and discipline practices they experienced as children from their own parents, they often have different parenting styles, which may create interparental conflict and confusion for children, exacerbating existing behavior problems. In addition, children's responses to particular discipline practices may depend on the extent to which these practices are normative in their community. For example, one study found a significant relationship between caregiver corporal punishment and child conduct problems among African American children in communities where physical discipline was rare, but no relationship between these two variables in communities where physical discipline was prevalent (Simons et al., 2002).

An emerging literature moves beyond consideration of parenting behavior to focus on dyadic dynamics in the parent-child relationship. Parent-child positive synchrony, defined as interaction that is mutually regulated, harmonious, and reciprocal (Harrist & Waugh, 2002), has been found to be significantly associated with children's adaptive self-regulation, particularly for those under six years of age (Davis, Bilms & Suveg, 2017).

Interparental Conflict

Interparental or couple conflict is associated with a wide range of child behavior problems. Research demonstrates that couple conflict increases children's emotional insecurity, which in turn leads to adjustment problems and psychopathology (Cummings & Davies, 2010). Alternatively, couple discord may lead to child behavior problems via its adverse impact on parenting practices or parent–child relationships, or via parental modeling of poor coping and conflict resolution skills. For example, couple discord can engender chronic distress or anger in parents, which may make them more reactive to their children's challenging behaviors.

Behavioral genetic research has demonstrated that interparental conflict contributes to child externalizing problems through increased parent-to-child hostility, with greater spillover of couple conflict to the father–child relationship than to the mother–child relationship (Harold et al., 2013). Couple conflict may also increase children's evocative effects on parenting. Research suggests that, as couple distress increases, mothers' negative parenting appears to be driven by genetically influenced child characteristics, whereas fathers' negative parenting is not (Ulbricht et al., 2013). The clinical implication of this finding is that marital distress can lead to increased differential parenting, polarization between parents in how they perceive the child, and scapegoating of the referred child.

Parental Depression

Depression in mothers is associated with children's internalizing problems, externalizing problems, and general psychopathology, with stronger effect sizes for younger children than older children (Goodman et al., 2011). Similar results have been found for depression in fathers, though paternal psychopathology may contribute to emotional and behavioral problems more during adolescence than in early childhood (Connell & Goodman, 2002). There are multiple complex mechanisms through which maternal depression may be associated with child psychopathology, including genetic, neurobiological (e.g., dysregulated stress regulation systems), social (e.g., modeling), and relational pathways. Relational mechanisms of influence include withdrawn and harsh or inconsistent parenting, and insecure mother–child attachment. Maternal depression also affects (and is affected by) the quality of the couple relationship and other relationships within and outside the family.

The negative impact of maternal depression on children's adjustment may be buffered by the child's relationships with other family members. For example, a healthy caregiver may protect the child by sustaining a good parent–child relationship, modeling constructive coping and affect regulation, and providing positive parenting. In addition, depressed mothers who experience emotional and instrumental support from their partners or parents may be more likely to engage in better-quality parenting than depressed mothers without support.

Maternal and paternal depressive symptoms are reciprocally linked with poor co-parenting over time (Tissot et al., 2017). Co-parenting is linked to, but distinct from, other aspects of couple relationship functioning. It is defined as the way in which two adults support each other and work as a team in childrearing tasks. Poor co-parenting is related to poor child adjustment beyond the effects of individual parenting or couple relationship quality (Teubert & Pinquart, 2010).

System-Wide Family Dynamics

Although there is more research on dyadic family processes (e.g., parenting, conflict within the couple) than on system-wide processes, a wealth of theory documents the important relationship between family functioning and child psychopathology. Processes that apply to the entire family are arguably more ecologically valid and capture more complexity than those confined to a single dyad embedded within the system. However, there is some variability across theories about what constitutes a healthy family and which dimensions of family functioning are most predictive of favorable child outcomes.

Observational research has established the influence of family cohesion (family members' emotional closeness to one another) and conflict on child behavior problems. For example, families of children with disruptive behavior problems demonstrated lower levels of cohesion and higher levels of conflict than families of children without these problems (Lindahl, 1998). In a longitudinal study of kindergartners, children from disengaged families showed higher initial levels of externalizing behavior problems and accelerated externalizing trajectories than children from cohesive and enmeshed families (Sturge-Apple, Davies, & Cummings, 2010). Children from enmeshed families were comparable with those from cohesive families in their initial levels of internalizing symptoms, but they exhibited greater increases in internalizing symptoms over time than children from cohesive families.

Broad Contextual Influences

Families are embedded in a number of nested contexts, including the neighborhood, caregiver and child peer networks, religious and school communities, systems of care, and macro-cultural systems related to socioeconomic status, culture, race, ethnicity, and nationality. Each of these contexts may contribute to child psychopathology directly. For example, children living in urban neighborhoods characterized by violent crime may suffer from traumatic stress due to exposure to community violence, and children living with parents who are undocumented immigrants may experience chronic anxiety due to fear of their deportation.

Neighborhood violence has been found to have wide-ranging detrimental effects for school age children (Osofsky, 1995), and neighborhood disadvantage (i.e., poverty and unemployment) has been associated with externalizing problems, particularly in early adolescence. For young children, however, neighborhood disadvantage may amplify the influence of family processes (e.g., parent–child conflict, parental stress, negative parenting practices) on their behavior problems. Neighborhood disadvantage also provides a context for children's association with neighborhood-based deviant peers, which then maintains or exacerbates antisocial behavior (Ingoldsby et al., 2006).

Economic hardship places families at risk for multiple difficulties associated with child psychopathology. According to the family stress model (Conger & Conger, 2002), economic hardship is linked to economic pressure (e.g., unmet material needs, inability to pay bills), which in turn leads to parental distress that results in interparental conflict. This distress and conflict then *spill over* into relationships with children via harsh and inconsistent parenting, resulting in children's behavior problems. Numerous studies across geographic settings and diverse racial and ethnic groups have found support for the family stress model in predicting child behavior problems during the elementary school years (e.g., Neppl, Senia, & Donnellan, 2016).

For the Medina family, contexts to explore include the parents' employment, parents' and children's friend networks, and the family's neighborhood and (if applicable) religious community. Perceived stressors at work and unmet needs for friendship in the community may contribute to the parents' anxiety and loneliness, constrain their parenting, and place a burden on family relationships. Conversely, resources and support for parents from their networks of colleagues and friends may partially offset the stress of parenting a child perceived as difficult.

Help-Seeking

Despite efforts over the past four decades to promote comprehensive, community-based, and culturally competent behavioral health (BH) services for children, racial and ethnic disparities in children's BH care persist in the United States. Minority children receive fewer and inferior BH services than their non-Latino white counterparts (Institute of Medicine, 2002). This disparity could reflect one or more of the following: (a) cultural differences in the perception of behavior problems and their causes, leading to under-recognition of psychiatric disorders;

(b) differences in help-seeking behavior and attitudes toward health-care providers; and (c) structural and sociopolitical constraints related to accessing services, such as poverty, lack of insurance, and insufficient availability of BH services in minority neighborhoods. Even when they are able to access care, minority children are significantly undertreated compared with their white counterparts, with linguistic minorities reporting worse care than English-speaking racial and ethnic minorities (Flores, 2009).

These findings have several implications for clinicians treating families. First, caregivers may have a different conceptualization of presenting problems than clinicians, as most theory and research in child development and family psychology is guided by an individually oriented, Eurocentric perspective (Stanton & Welsh, 2011). For example, a mother may perceive a five-year-old boy's verbal aggression toward her as a demonstration of his lack of respect, best quashed with a strong show of force, rather than a protest that is best ignored. Second, caregivers may have difficulty trusting BH providers based on their own family history or the collective experience of their ethnic minority group; they may prefer to seek help for the child from a pastor or preacher rather than from a psychologist. Some minority caregivers seeking BH services for their children have had negative or, at best, mixed experiences with helping professionals, resulting in reluctant engagement in treatment, or over-reporting or under-reporting of child behavior problems. Finally, the sociopolitical factors (e.g., poverty) limiting caregivers' access to BH services may also constrain the quality of their parenting, contributing to expectations that the clinician will judge them negatively.

It is often the case that different family members have divergent or conflicting ideas about the nature and cause of the child's problem, the need for a BH evaluation, and the most appropriate or effective solution. These ideas may be based on culturally influenced beliefs or values, or on individual or collective experiences of privilege, oppression, or marginalization. Culturally influenced beliefs and values to explore in the Medina family include those related to childrearing, help-seeking, and the family's relationships with extended family, friends or colleagues, and the community.

Systems of Care

Children receive BH services in many different service settings, including schools, child welfare, juvenile justice, mental health providers, and pediatric primary care. These sectors of the child BH system are often administratively and fiscally segregated, leading to an uneven and uncoordinated patchwork of service options (Kazak et al., 2010). Despite national efforts to promote a coordinated network of community-based services for children with psychopathology, most BH services for children have not been incorporated into these integrated systems of care (Osofsky & Lieberman, 2011). Therefore, it is incumbent upon the individual clinician to determine whether children presenting for evaluation are also receiving BH services from their school counselors, pediatricians, or clinicians contracted with juvenile justice or the statutory child protection agency.

There is little doubt that simultaneous BH service delivery across systems complicates assessment and treatment of child psychopathology. Clinicians from many professional disciplines are ethically bound to avoid duplication of services. Yet, children may demonstrate different behaviors in different settings, and interventions are best delivered in the natural context most salient to the presenting problem. For example, an intervention targeting social skill deficits (e.g., group therapy) may be best implemented in a school setting, whereas treatment addressing parent–child conflict is best delivered in the context of home- or clinic-based family therapy. It is ethically plausible for a child to simultaneously receive school- or home-based BH services from two different clinicians as long as each of the interventions targets a different problem or etiological process within a shared case formulation, and the two clinicians communicate with one another to coordinate their care. Lack of communication and coordination places the clinicians at risk for working at cross purposes, jeopardizing the relationship of the family with another service provider, and contributing to the family's burden of care.

One of the most common partnerships in BH service delivery is the collaboration between the therapist and the medical provider managing the child's medication. In many cases, the medical provider is the child's pediatrician; indeed, half of *well-care* appointments in pediatric primary care address behavioral concerns (Cassidy & Jellinek, 1998). However, many pediatricians feel unprepared to accurately diagnose and treat child psychopathology. Psychiatrists, particularly those boarded in child and adolescent psychiatry, have the broad base of knowledge and advanced clinical skillset to effectively provide pharmacological interventions to children with a variety of psychiatric disorders; unfortunately, there are not enough child psychiatrists to meet service needs in the United States, particularly in the rural areas. Many children are prescribed medication for emotional or behavioral disorders by psychiatrists without specialized training in child development, or by primary health-care providers, which may contribute to troubling trends in polypharmacy (i.e., the simultaneous use of multiple medications to treat a single disorder) (Comer, Olfson, & Mojtabai, 2010) and inappropriate prioritization of pharmacological over nonpharmacological intervention. Clinicians treating child behavior problems should communicate with the child's medical provider to: (a) develop a consensus about the diagnosis and treatment plan, (b) avoid or manage conflicting advice to the family, and (c) work collaboratively in the service of quality patient care, consistent with competencies for interprofessional collaborative practice (Interprofessional Education Collaborative Expert Panel, 2011).

Although children's BH is generally served by communication and coordination across service systems, sometimes a system is not a good fit for a given child or family, and the poor fit may contribute to the child's presenting problems. An example would be a school that does not recognize or provide services for a child's special education needs, or a child welfare worker who negatively evaluates parents due to their culturally influenced communication practices. In these cases, the clinician may assist the family in finding a school that provides a better fit for their needs, or in educating the child welfare worker about the influence of the family's culture on how the parents communicate with community gatekeepers.

In the case of the Medina family, the clinician will need to coordinate BH care with Elena's school personnel and pediatrician. It will be important to assess the parents' and child's perceived relationships with both the school system and the pediatrician, without creating or reinforcing tension among family members or between the family and the school or health-care provider. The pediatrician's and school personnel's perceptions and observations also may aid the clinician in understanding Elena's presenting problems.

Conclusion

Etiological influences operate at multiple levels (biological, familial, community or social, sociocultural) and interact in complex ways to produce and maintain psychopathology in childhood. Empirical research has yielded advances in knowledge about the most influential causal pathways; however, few studies consider multiple factors across levels or disentangle the effects of heritability from environment. Another limitation is the small effect sizes found for significant associations between family processes and child outcomes in many studies, limiting the clinical applicability of the findings. For example, the documented association between harsh parenting and child behavior problems does not necessarily suggest that parenting is the most important or influential etiological factor to target for intervention with a particular family. Normal and pathological child behavior result from the dynamic interaction among multiple risk and protective factors over time and across developmental domains (biological, emotional, cognitive, social). In any family presenting for treatment, discovery of the multiple and interacting mechanisms contributing to the child's behavior problems will depend on a comprehensive assessment of the child in his or her nested sociocultural contexts. Nevertheless, theory and research on systemic processes associated with child psychopathology can guide the clinician in asking questions, with the goal of developing a systemic conceptualization that can drive treatment.

References

Cassidy, L. J., & Jellinek, M. S. (1998). Approaches to recognition and management of childhood psychiatric disorders in pediatric primary care. *Pediatric Clinics, 45*(5), 1037–1052.

Cecil, C. A. M., Barker, E. D., Jaffee, S. R., & Viding, E. (2012). Association between maladaptive parenting and child self-control over time: Cross-lagged study using a monozygotic twin difference design. *The British Journal of Psychiatry, 201*(4), 291–297.

Comer, J. S., Olfson, M., & Mojtabai, R. (2010). National trends in child and adolescent psychotropic polypharmacy in office-based practice, 1996–2007. *Journal of the American Academy of Child & Adolescent Psychiatry, 49*(10), 1001–1010.

Conger, R. D., & Conger, K. J. (2002). Resilience in Midwestern families: Selected findings from the first decade of a prospective, longitudinal study. *Journal of Marriage and Family, 64*(2), 361–373.

Connell, A. M., & Goodman, S. H. (2002). The association between Psychopathology in fathers versus mothers and children's internalizing and externalizing behavior problems: A meta-analysis. *Psychological Bulletin, 128*(5), 746–773.

Cummings, E. M., & Davies, P. T. (2010). *Marital conflict and children: An emotional security perspective.* New York, NY and London, UK: Guilford Press.

Davis, M., Bilms, J., & Suveg, C. (2017). In sync and in control: A meta-analysis of parent-child positive behavioral synchrony and youth self-regulation. *Family Process, 56* (4), 962–980.

De Bellis, M. D., & Zisk, A. (2014). The biological effects of childhood trauma. *Child and Adolescent Psychiatric Clinics of North America, 23*(2), 185–222.

Eddy, J. M., Leve, L. D., & Fagot, B. I. (2001). Coercive family processes: A replication and extension of Patterson's coercion model. *Aggressive Behavior, 27*(1), 14–25.

Ehrenreich-May, J., & Chu, B. C. (2014). *Transdiagnostic treatments for children and adolescents: Principles and practice.* New York, NY: Guilford Press.

Eley, T. C., Napolitano, M., Lau, J. Y. F., & Gregory, A. M. (2010). Does childhood anxiety evoke maternal control? A genetically informed study. *Journal of Child Psychology and Psychiatry, 51*(7), 772–779.

Flores, G. (2009). Devising, implementing, and evaluating interventions to eliminate health care disparities in minority children. *Pediatrics, 124*(Suppl 3), S214–S223.

Goodman, S. H., Rouse, M. H., Connell, A. M., Broth, M. R., Hall, C. M., & Heyward, D. (2011). Maternal depression and child psychopathology: A meta-analytic review. *Clinical Child and Family Psychology Review, 14*(1), 1–27.

Harold, G. T., Leve, L. D., Elam, K. K., Thapar, A., Neiderhiser, J. M., Natsuaki, M. N., Shaw, D. S., & Reiss, D. (2013). The nature of nurture: Disentangling passive genotype–environment correlation from family relationship influences on children's externalizing problems. *Journal of Family Psychology, 27*(1), 12–21.

Harrist, A. W., & Waugh, R. M. (2002). Dyadic synchrony: Its structure and function in children's development. *Developmental Review, 22*, 555–592.

Ingoldsby, E. M., Shaw, D. S., Winslow, E., Schonberg, M., Gilliom, M., & Criss, M. M. (2006). Neighborhood disadvantage, parent–child conflict, neighborhood peer relationships, and early antisocial behavior problem trajectories. *Journal of Abnormal Child Psychology, 34*(3), 293–309.

Institute of Medicine. (2002). *Unequal treatment: Confronting racial and ethnic disparities in health care.* Washington, DC: The National Academies Press.

Interprofessional Education Collaborative Expert Panel. (2011). *Core competencies for interprofessional collaborative practice: Report of an expert panel.* Washington, DC: Interprofessional Education Collaborative Expert Panel.

Kagan, J., Reznick, J. S., Clarke, C., Snidman, N., & Garcia-Coll, C. (1984). Behavioral inhibition to the unfamiliar. *Child Development, 55*(6), 2212–2225.

Kazak, A. E., Hoagwood, K., Weisz, J. R., Hood, K., Kratochwill, T. R., Vargas, L. A., & Banez, G. A. (2010). A meta-systems approach to evidence-based practice for children and adolescents. *American Psychologist, 65*(2), 85–97.

Leve, L. D., Harold, G. T., Ge, X., Neiderhiser, J. M., Shaw, D., Scaramella, L. V., & Reiss, D. (2009). Structured parenting of toddlers at high versus low genetic risk: Two pathways to child problems. *Journal of the American Academy of Child & Adolescent Psychiatry, 48*(11), 1102–1109.

Lindahl, K. M. (1998). Family process variables and children's disruptive behavior problems. *Journal of Family Psychology, 12*(3), 420–436.

McLeod, B. D., Wood, J. J., & Weisz, J. R. (2007). Examining the association between parenting and childhood anxiety: A meta-analysis. *Clinical Psychology Review, 27*(2), 155–172.

McLeod, B. D., Weisz, J. R., & Wood, J. J. (2007). Examining the association between parenting and childhood depression: A meta-analysis. *Clinical Psychology Review, 27*(8), 986–1003.

Narusyte, J., Neiderhiser, J. M., D'onofrio, B. M., Reiss, D., Spotts, E. L., Ganiban, J., & Lichtenstein, P. (2008). Testing different types of genotype-environment correlation: An extended children-of-twins model. *Developmental Psychology, 44*(6), 1591–1603.

Neppl, T. K., Senia, J. M., & Donnellan, M. B. (2016). Effects of economic hardship: Testing the family stress model over time. *Journal of Family Psychology, 30*(1), 12–21.

Osofsky, J.D. (1995). The effect of exposure to violence on young children. *American Psychologist, 50*(9), 782-788.

Osofsky, J. D., & Lieberman, A. F. (2011). A call for integrating a mental health perspective into systems of care for abused and neglected infants and young children. *American Psychologist, 66*(2), 120–128.

Patterson, G. R. (1976). The aggressive child: victim and architect of a coercive system. In E. J. Mash, L. A. Hamerlynck, & L. C. Handy (Eds.), *Behavior modification and families* (pp. 267–316). New York, NY: Brunner/Mazel.

Rothbaum, F., & Weisz, J. R. (1994). Parental caregiving and child externalizing behavior in nonclinical samples: A meta-analysis. *Psychological Bulletin, 116*(1), 55–74.

Silk, J. S., Sessa, F. M., Morris, A. S., Steinberg, L., & Avenevoli, S. (2004). Neighborhood cohesion as a buffer against hostile maternal parenting. *Journal of Family Psychology, 18*(1), 135–146.

Simons, R. L., Lin, K.-H., Gordon, L. C., Brody, G. H., Murry, V., & Conger, R. D. (2002). Community differences in the association between parenting practices and child conduct problems. *Journal of Marriage and Family, 64*(2), 331–345.

Slagt, M., Dubas, J. S., Dekovic, M., & van Aken, M. A. G. (2016). Differences in sensitivity to parenting depending on child temperament: A meta-analysis. *Psychological Bulletin, 142*(10), 1068–1110.

Stanton, M., & Welsh, R. K. (2011). *Specialty competencies in couple and family psychology.* Oxford, UK: Oxford University Press.

Sturge-Apple, M. L., Davies, P. T., & Cummings, E. M. (2010). Typologies of family functioning and children's adjustment during the early school years. *Child Development, 81*(4), 1320–1335.

Teubert, D., & Pinquart, M. (2010). The association between coparenting and child adjustment: A meta-analysis. *Parenting: Science and Practice, 10*(4), 286–307.

Tissot, H., Favez, N., Ghisletta, P., Frascarolo, F., & Despland, J.-N. (2017). A longitudinal study of parental depressive symptoms and coparenting in the first 18 months. *Family Process, 56*(2), 445–458.

Ulbricht, J. A., Ganiban, J. M., Button, T. M. M., Feinberg, M., Reiss, D., & Neiderhiser, J. M. (2013). Marital adjustment as a moderator for genetic and environmental influences on parenting. *Journal of Family Psychology, 27*(1), 42–52.

CHAPTER 3

Family Assessment and Systemic Case Conceptualization

The purpose of an assessment is to gain enough information about the causes and context of a presenting problem to develop a case formulation and treatment plan. The distinguishing feature of a Couple and Family Psychology (CFP)assessment is its grounding in systemic concepts and related knowledge. Guided by theory and research (see Chapter 2), a CFP assessment ultimately yields a systemic case conceptualization, which is the conceptual map that will guide treatment for a given child and family. In addition, assessment provides the context for the development of a systemic alliance, a key component of CFP practice. The following sections describe the nature and scope of CFP assessment methods using a client-centered perspective, apply these methods and perspective to the Medina family, and propose a systemic conceptualization of the case.

Nature and Scope of CFP Assessment Methods

CFP assessment encompasses a broad range of methods and content domains across the system levels of individuals, dyads, families, and their broader contexts. For child behavior problems, assessment includes the perspectives of the referred child, the parents, siblings, teachers, and sometimes, other involved adults (e.g., health-care providers, aftercare staff). CFP assessment examines not only the referred child's developmental history and presenting problem, but also family structure and composition, relationships among family members, specific family processes (e.g., communication, problem-solving, parenting, emotional expression, organization), the family's relationships with other relevant systems (e.g., school), and broader cultural and contextual factors influencing proximal family processes. The particular content areas selected for exploration depend on the nature of the presenting problem. Positive and negative aspects of relationships are evaluated separately, as they function somewhat independently of one another (Fincham & Linfield, 1997); for example, conflict between siblings does not suggest a lack of positive connection.

There is no *gold standard* method used in CFP assessment. The most common CFP methods for evaluating child behavior problems are the clinical interview, standardized assessment instruments, behavioral observations of family interactions, and information-gathering from school staff and other care providers. The information obtained by one method is not always consistent with data obtained by another. As a result, most clinicians rely on more than one method, looking for consensus among the data in developing a systemic case formulation. Typically, the assessment is conducted in one to three sessions by a single clinician, with family member attendance determined in part by the method chosen.

Clinical Interview

Although a clinical interview of the client is the mainstay of all behavioral health (BH) assessment, it is complicated in child assessment by children's developmental constraints, dependence on parents, and lack of experience or comfort in talking with strangers about their experiences. Thus, clinicians have to rely in part on data obtained from parents, which requires consideration of context; after all, parents' observations of the child's behavior are influenced by their relationships with the child and other family members. Accordingly, the clinician conducting a CFP assessment makes thoughtful decisions about who to interview in the presence of whom. Should the child be interviewed alone or with the parent(s) present? Should the parents be interviewed in the child's presence? These decisions have important implications for how the family and the clinician define the problem, but also for what type of family interactions the clinician may observe during the interview. In many cases, an individual interview of the child may communicate to family members that it is the child's behavior alone that is problematic. On the other hand, discussion of the presenting problem with the entire family may elicit negative parent–child interactions and prevent opportunities for positive interactions. There is some controversy about the necessity to interview the entire family in a CFP assessment; evaluation of key dyads (e.g., parent–child interactions, co-parenting relationship) may be more useful and expedient than assessing the family as a whole (Bray, 2009).

Decisions about who to interview are complicated in the case of separated or divorced parents. If parents in separate households share custody of the child or the noncustodial parent has regular visitation, both should be interviewed as part of the assessment, though the clinician may choose to interview them separately. It is best to negotiate the involvement of the second parent before or at the beginning of the first assessment session; otherwise, a clinician's request to interview the other parent may be perceived by the presenting parent as a reaction to the interview or observed family interaction.

The questions asked during a clinical interview depend in part on the clinician's conceptual model of how contextual factors could be related to the presenting problem. Given the wide acceptance of behavioral theory among clinicians who treat children, parents are often asked about the history and context of the child's challenging behavior, including its antecedents and consequences. In a CFP assessment, a clinical interview also includes questions about the impact of the child's challenging behavior on the parents and on the child's family and peer relationships.

A distinguishing feature of a CFP assessment is the clinician's inquiry into family patterns without referencing the presenting problem, often before the problem is even brought up. The clinician typically asks circular and narrative questions about family patterns in the context of a family interview so that all members can hear and react to one another's responses, providing a rich tapestry of perspectives and observational data. Circular questions (Fleuridas, Nelson, & Rosenthal, 1986) are designed to reveal relationship patterns: Who is closest to whom in the family? Who argues the most with whom? Who notices first when Mom or Dad is upset? Which parent has the most rules? Clinicians seek responses from children before parents to minimize parental influence on children's answers, and model acceptance of each member's perspective, setting the stage for a systemic alliance with the family. Narrative questions ask family members to reflect on their beliefs. (What does it mean to you to be a good mother? What is the difference between being a perfect mother and *good enough*?) They are ideal for seeking information about how cultural factors are related to salient family processes (e.g., what does it mean to be Jewish in this family: how does it affect how you discipline the children?).

When questions are asked about the presenting problem, they tend to be solution focused (e.g., In what situations is her behavior less of a problem? What would be the smallest possible step toward improvement?) to facilitate problem-solving and build a therapeutic alliance. Circular, narrative, and solution-focused questions are considered interventive (Tomm, 1987) as they invite family members to reflect on their beliefs and feelings, or view problems and relationships differently, potentially leading to therapeutic change.

Self-Report Instruments

There are many reliable and valid self-report instruments that assess parent and child perceptions of child behavior, parent characteristics (e.g., parenting stress), and family functioning. Self-report instruments are easy to administer, offer an economical way of obtaining and comparing different family members' perspectives, and can be repeated over time to document symptom improvement. Norm-based instruments can help clinicians determine the clinical significance of presenting problems or parent characteristics. Clinicians assessing child behavior problems often use a broad-band parent-report instrument such as the Child Behavior Checklist (Achenbach, 1991) or the Behavior Assessment System for Children (Reynolds & Kamphaus, 2015), or a narrow-band measure assessing the presenting symptom (e.g., disruptive behavior). Ideally, each instrument is completed by both parents for the purpose of comparison; parents often have divergent or conflicting views that may impede problem resolution.

Self-report instruments are available to assess general family functioning, as well as specific domains, including family communication and problem-solving, emotional cohesion, and organization (see Hamilton & Carr, 2016, for a review). These instruments were developed primarily for use in research, but several are suitable for clinical use. Information obtained from one individual on these instruments may not accurately reflect the functioning of the entire family; therefore, family members' responses are combined (averaged or weighted) to yield information about family functioning. A number of criticisms have been leveled against these self-report measures. Each instrument is based on a particular conceptual model of family functioning that: (a) has not necessarily been validated with families from diverse ethnic backgrounds, and (b) may not be consistent with recent scientific findings on family processes associated with child psychopathology. In addition, these instruments do not always discriminate between clinical and normal samples, or between different types of family dysfunction (Grotevant & Carlson, 1989). Finally, they are designed to be completed by family members over age 10 to 12, limiting their usefulness with children.

Observational Methods

In contrast to self-report instruments, observational methods represent a trained professional's view of the family. The clinician decides *what* should be observed (i.e., which specific task or discussion), *who* should be present (e.g., mother–child dyad or entire family), *where* the observation should take place (e.g., home or clinic), and *how* it should be observed (e.g., informally or with a specific coding system). Observational methods in CFP consist of: (a) *informal evaluations*, in which the clinician observes natural or elicited family interactions; (b) *clinical rating scales*, which provide a structured format for evaluation of specific systemic constructs; or (c) *coding schemes*, in which trained observers use a microanalytic or macroanalytic rating system to evaluate key aspects of family interaction.

All CFP assessment incorporates informal or qualitative observational methods. Beginning during the first interview and continuing throughout therapy, the clinician observes family interactions to draw conclusions about family relationships and organization, and to make hypotheses about how family processes influence the presenting problem. Observational data may be verbal, nonverbal (who sits next to whom, eye signals encouraging or discouraging others to speak), or paraverbal (voice tone).

Observed interactions occur spontaneously in the course of a clinical interview, or can be elicited by a specific task directed by the clinician.

A common assessment task is the family sculpture, in which each family member is asked to physically place other family members in positions and proximity to one another to represent his or her current view of the family. All family members are given a turn to make a sculpture, and each member's sculpture is accepted by the clinician without judgment or questioning. One or more family members may be asked to sculpt how they would "like their family to be" (ideal family sculpture). Family members' sculptures and reactions to one another's sculptures convey information about shared and divergent family perceptions in a short period of time; ideal family sculptures can be translated into treatment goals (e.g., greater closeness in the family). As young children do not possess the abstract thinking required to represent relationships by configuring people in space, their sculptures may portray a slice of family life (e.g., children arguing while parents cook dinner). Nevertheless, their contributions can be illuminating, and inviting them to complete a sculpture conveys that all members' perspectives are important.

Other family interaction tasks are designed to elicit the child's challenging behavior or presenting problem with family members present. For example, a child with oppositional behavior can be invited to play a rule-bound game with the family and clinician, and then directed by the parents to put away the game pieces without help. A child reported to have poor frustration tolerance or performance anxiety can be asked to complete an assembly task (e.g., puzzle, blocks) perceived as difficult. These tasks allow the clinician to observe the family interactions within which the child's difficult behavior is embedded. It is important to remember that different tasks elicit different types of behavior and interaction patterns; problem-solving and conflict resolution tasks may elicit hostility and discord, whereas discussion of a child's recent loss or disappointment tends to produce parental warmth and support. Employing multiple tasks can lead to a more complete picture of how the family functions in different situations.

There are a number of clinical rating scales designed for observational family assessment (for a review, see Hampson & Beavers, 2004). Several correspond with similarly named self-report instruments that are based on a particular model of family functioning. These rating scales are completed by a trained clinician after conducting or observing a detailed family interview or an elicited discussion task. Clinical rating scales yield psychometrically more reliable and valid data on family functioning than self-report instruments, but they require training and knowledge about the relevant conceptual model of family functioning.

The genogram, though not a formal clinical rating scale, is a useful method for obtaining and pictorially documenting information about family relationships over at least three generations (McGoldrick, Gerson, & Petry, 2008). Although the clinical use of a genogram does not necessarily influence conceptualization and treatment of presenting problems, it is a helpful tool for organizing and discussing historical patterns in the family (e.g., gender-based parenting styles), as well as the impact of historical events (e.g., immigration, death of parent) on family relationships. Given the sensitivity of some historical family information, the genogram is best conducted without young children present.

Coding schemes differ from clinical rating scales in that they measure more narrowly defined individual behaviors (e.g., warmth, hostility) or dyadic processes elicited in a family interaction task, usually observed by the clinician from a video recording or behind a one-way mirror. As coding systems require extensive training to achieve reliable and valid results, they are used more in research than in clinical practice. However, some of these coding systems can be useful in CFP assessment. For example, the Dyadic Parent–Child Interaction Coding System (Eyberg et al., 2014), developed for use in Parent–Child Interaction Therapy (McNeil & Hembree-Kigin, 2011), documents sequenced patterns of parent–child interaction (i.e., parent command, child compliance or noncompliance, whether parent gives a labeled praise for compliance) relevant to the assessment of oppositional behavior.

Client-Centered Perspective

A key component in the CFP assessment competency domain is a client-centered perspective, characterized as an attitude rather than knowledge or a skill. Clinicians use a client-centered perspective when they conduct the assessment in a manner that is meaningful and immediately useful to families, and honors the complexity and dignity of the human experience (Stanton & Welsh, 2011), including clients' cultural identities and family forms. This attitude also conveys respect for clients as fellow human beings, with strengths as well as weaknesses. For example, clinicians demonstrate a client-centered perspective when they negotiate with the parents how the assessment will be justified and introduced to the children. Clinicians should try to get to know family members apart from the presenting problem, and give them an opportunity to demonstrate cooperation as well as discord in assessment sessions. Parents should not be asked to discuss sensitive information (e.g., their finances or health) in the presence of young children, unless they give permission for these inquiries. A client-centered perspective is also characterized by humility in interpreting and presenting assessment data. For example, clinicians avoid unnecessary jargon, consider their own biases in interpreting observational data, and avoid using language that indicates more certainty than is warranted by the data. If the referred child has a previous diagnosis, parents should be asked whether they accept the diagnosis, as well as whether the diagnosis has been helpful or not helpful in resolving the presenting problems. Doing so communicates respect for differences of opinion and demonstrates a collaborative relationship with the parents.

A client-centered perspective requires the clinician to consider the developmental needs and cultural identities of all family members, the developmental stage of the family, and the family's cultural context (for more discussion of cultural diversity, see Chapter 6). Most young children have difficulty remaining seated and involved in a group discussion for a lengthy period; therefore, family interviews should include engaging tasks or games suited to the youngest members' developmental needs. Parents' culturally influenced beliefs about when and how children should speak or handle toys should be accepted and respected. For example, a child who picks up a toy in the office may be immediately instructed by the parent to put it down. In this case, the clinician should avoid countermanding the parent's directive and instead support the parent's instruction, clarifying that there will be an opportunity to play with toys later or at another time.

Sometimes a client-centered perspective appears to conflict with the goal of developing a systemic alliance, or with the foundational competency of fostering positive interpersonal relationships. When parents attempt to shame or scold children about their behavior (e.g., "tell the doctor why you were kicked out of school!"), the clinician can feel torn between allowing the discussion to naturally unfold (client-centered perspective) at the expense of appearing to side with the parents, and re-directing the discussion to be less shaming at the expense of appearing to side with the child. A similar challenge to a client-centered perspective emerges when parents share developmentally questionable interpretations of the child's behavior, such as when a mother insists that her four-year-old daughter's tantrums convey a lack of *respect* or that she lies in a manipulative and planned manner. If the clinician chooses to educate the parent about more developmentally realistic interpretations at this time, there may be damage to the developing therapeutic alliance. A better strategy might be to explore the mother's understanding and experiences of *respect* in parent–child relationships, and how she might teach her daughter to *tell the truth*.

Application of Assessment Methods to Case

The first assessment session was held with the parents only. Karen took the lead in discussing her concerns about Elena's behavior, and Emilio voiced his agreement. Both appeared anxious during the interview. Emilio checked his phone a few times, earning irritated glances from his wife. Karen looked down or away often, smoothed her hair, and laughed nervously when describing the intensity of her daughter's tantrums. When the parents were asked to describe their son, Emilio immediately offered "he's a good boy," recounting Julian's successes in school and sports. Karen echoed his sentiments, adding that Julian has always been more easygoing than his sister. When the parents were asked whom Elena's "personality" reminded them of, Emilio looked at Karen pointedly. Karen sighed and said "my mother," later clarifying that she had not spoken to her mother in months, and had not visited in years. She reported that she got along better with her father, who had remarried after her parents' divorce. Emilio said he had good relationships with both of his parents, though he acknowledged that his father "had a temper." He said his parents immigrated from Puerto Rico to the United States when he was 12, and that "people in my family talk on the phone to each other every day." This statement earned a snort from Karen, who added: "they'd move in if we let them." Emilio agreed, adding that his parents visit for a week or more every few months.

Discussion of the co-parenting relationship revealed that Karen has the primary responsibility for managing the children. She returned to a full-time work schedule almost two years ago when Julian started kindergarten, but cut her hours to two days per week when Elena's behavior problems worsened a few months ago. When she needs help in managing Elena's oppositional behavior, she calls for Emilio to step in, which he does without hesitation. However, he often loses his temper with Elena or gives her a punishment that is difficult for Karen to enforce, causing tension in their marital relationship. In addition, the couple's demanding jobs and the children's busy extracurricular schedules cause Karen and Emilio to feel "exhausted," though Karen clarified that she is less exhausted on work days. They have not gone out together without the children in several months, partly because they do not trust Elena to "act right" with a babysitter. At the end of the interview, the clinician described her systemic approach to understanding child behavior problems, negotiated an assessment plan and how to explain to the children why the assessment was needed, and obtained a signed release to gather relevant information from Elena's teacher and pediatrician.

Each parent completed a Child Behavior Checklist (CBCL) and an Eyberg Child Behavior Inventory (ECBI; Eyberg & Pincus, 1999) for Elena, as well as a Parenting Stress Index (PSI; Abidin, 1995). Their ECBI ratings yielded elevated and convergent scores for Elena, suggesting significant problems with oppositional and disruptive behavior. Parent ratings on the CBCL produced significantly elevated scores on subscales assessing somatic complaints and aggressive behavior. Karen's ratings also yielded an elevated score on the subscale assessing anxious or depressed behavior, but Emilio's did not. All other CBCL subscale scores were in the normal range. Both parents' total scores on the PSI suggested high levels of parenting stress related to raising Elena, with higher levels of stress for Karen than for Emilio.

The second assessment session was held with the entire family. Karen and Julian sat together on a sofa, Emilio sat in an adjacent chair, and Elena initially sat in her father's lap. After a few minutes, Elena moved to sit next to her brother; in response, Emilio pointed to the chair next to his and told his daughter firmly to sit there, which she did, albeit reluctantly. The clinician *led introductions and gave the explanation of her role that was previously negotiated with the parents ("I help kids and families get along better"). She asked the children some questions about their lives apart from the presenting problem, engaging both in a discussion of their favorite activity. Then, the clinician asked a series of circular questions (e.g., Who is the quietest person in the family? Who has more rules, Mom or Dad? Which two argue the most?). Both children eagerly offered answers while their parents listened. The parents often agreed with the children's perspectives, and when they disagreed with one or both of the children, they did so respectfully. Elena appeared irritated when her parents disagreed with her, but became overtly angry when they supported Julian's perspective. The clinician successfully redirected Elena by moving to the next question. The family agreed that Elena is the loudest, Mom is the quietest, Dad has fewer rules, but a hotter temper than Mom, and the most arguments occur between Elena and Julian or Karen.*

The clinician then invited family members to do a family sculpture, starting with Julian, then Elena, and then each of the parents. Julian's sculpture featured his father coaching his baseball team while his mother and sister cheered for him on the sidelines. Elena placed her mother next to her brother on one end of the couch, "helping him with his homework," and her father seated at a nearby table "on his laptop." She hesitated about where to put herself in the sculpture, ultimately sitting on the end of the couch closest to her father, "playing on my tablet." Karen's sculpture showed herself trying to separate Julian and Elena, who were fighting, while Emilio sat in another room "working." Emilio's sculpture featured Elena "stamping her foot and screaming" while Julian stood nearby covering his ears. He placed himself next to his wife, facing Elena, his finger pointed at her, "giving her consequences." He then sighed and said to Elena: "we don't want it to be like this." The clinician invited Emilio to do a sculpture that showed how he would like his family to be. He brought both children to stand near the couple so that the family formed a tight circle, and drew his wife closer to him. The kids pressed in, and placed their arms around adjacent members' waists, with the parents following suit.

The family members were then asked to say one thing they like and one thing they want to change about the family. All members identified similar strengths (have fun together, play games, Mom's baking, Dad's chicken and rice). Elena wanted more family trips and fun activities, and the parents wanted more cooperation and less arguing from the kids. During the last part of the session, the clinician and family played a card game together. Both parents were observed to smile and show more patience with Julian than with Elena during game play.

In the third assessment session, the clinician conducted a clinical interview with Elena and verbally administered the Multidimensional Anxiety Scale for Children (MASC 2, March 2000), a self-report instrument assessing anxiety symptoms. Elena denied symptoms of depression, suicidal ideation, and exposure to traumatic events. She admitted "going from 1 to 10" very quickly when upset, but did not think she got upset more than most kids her age. She indicated she had many friends, and denied that she bullied or was bullied by others. She said she had missed school due to tummy aches. When asked what was the worst and scariest thing that had ever happened to her, she said she overheard an argument between her parents in which her father threatened to "move out." It happened several months ago, and she has not heard another argument or talked with her parents about what she heard. Elena's MASC ratings yielded a total T-score of 71, reflecting significant anxiety across the domains of physical symptoms, harm avoidance, and separation. Her social anxiety domain score was not elevated.

Discussion with Elena's teacher revealed that Elena is an excellent student, earning As and Bs, with good relationships with teachers and peers. The teacher reported that Elena is frequently tardy, and she often asks to visit the school nurse due to stomach aches. With three months of school left in the academic year, Elena has missed 24 days. Over the past two weeks, she has attended only four days, all Thursdays and Fridays.

Systemic Conceptualization of Case

Stanton and Welsh (2011) identify three phases of case conceptualization: (a) problem formulation, in which family problems are described; (b) case formulation, in which the problems are explained according to a systemic theory or framework; and (c) treatment formulation (see Chapter 4), in which a plan for problem resolution is prescribed. When the referred client is a child, systemic conceptualizations also incorporate theory and science related to individual development. Child development includes sensitive periods during which the effect of experience on the brain is particularly strong. In addition, different developmental tasks and phases may trigger different parent sensitivities and elicit different responses.

Problem Formulation

The presenting problems for the Medina family are Elena's school refusal and oppositional behavior at home. However, the assessment revealed a number of other problems as well: tension in the co-parenting relationship, high levels of parenting stress for Karen, sibling conflict, Elena's anxiety and poor coping skills, Emilio's *hot temper*, Elena's strained relationships with both parents, and limited family and peer support for Karen. The assessment also indicated a number of family strengths: parental warmth and involvement in the children's activities, parents' developmentally appropriate expectations and communication with both kids, and cooperation between siblings when not in competition with one another.

Problem formulation often includes a psychiatric diagnosis for the child. Sharing the diagnosis with the family can be difficult, as the parents' categories of understanding child behavior may conflict with the descriptions of human experience embedded in the *Diagnostic and Statistical Mmanual of Mental Disorders* (American Psychiatric Association, 2013). Sometimes the clinician and the parents disagree about a diagnosis. Although agreement about the diagnosis is not always necessary for treatment, the clinician and the parents should agree about the target problems. In the case of the Medina family, the parents may agree with the diagnosis of oppositional defiant disorder, but not with the diagnosis of an anxiety disorder. However, for treatment to succeed, at a minimum they would need to recognize that Elena has difficulty making good decisions when she is under stress.

Case Formulation

The essential task in case formulation is to identify the developmental, family, and broader contextual processes that contribute to or maintain the presenting problem, or impede problem resolution. For the Medina family, both the school refusal and oppositional behavior are related, at least in part, to Elena's anxiety. Elena may act out and refuse to obey her parents to avoid situations she perceives as uncomfortable or threatening. Similarly, Elena may avoid school to escape stressful school experiences and to manage her anxiety about family relationships. The initial somatic complaints causing her to miss school elicited a nurturing response from Karen. Over time, however, Karen has become frustrated and despondent, and Emilio has become impatient and angry, about Elena's continued school avoidance.

Contextual factors contributing to Elena's anxiety are her parents' inconsistent and unpredictable reactions to her disruptive behavior, her perception that her mother is unhappy and her father may leave the family, and her growing conviction that both parents prefer to spend time with her brother more than with her. Elena's challenging behaviors have caused her parents to expect (and experience) fewer positive interactions with her, and to suffer from increased parental stress in the context of limited peer and family support (Karen), a demanding job (Emilio), uneven division of responsibility for child behavior management, and possibly divergent or conflicting beliefs about parenting based on Emilio's and Karen's different familial and cultural experiences. The strained parent–child relationships and increased parenting stress exacerbate existing marital discord, and all of these factors impede problem resolution. Increased communication with the school system and the pediatrician add to the parental burden and place even greater demands on the strained co-parenting relationship.

At the end of the assessment phase, the clinician discussed the case formulation with the parents, providing a developmentally appropriate and brief explanation to the children. The clinician told Elena: "I think you don't like to go to school sometimes because you are not comfortable there when you feel worried, and you seem to be worried a lot. Is that right?" After Elena accepted this explanation, the clinician continued: "the problem is that the more you stay home from school, the more upset your parents get, and the more you feel that they like your brother more than you." Elena nodded, saying her parents were *nicer* to Julian than to her. The clinician continued:

> Another problem with missing school is that the more you stay out, the harder it is to go back, and everybody—you included—believes that it is best for kids to go to school. Your parents want

you to go to school every day, and they want you to feel safe in school. They also want to fix the things you're worried about. That's why they've asked me for help.

This explanation can lead to a discussion of the treatment formulation (see Chapter 4).

Conclusion

Assessment of child behavior problems from a systemic perspective is complex due to the number of individuals and contexts involved, as well as the data supporting bidirectional influences of parenting on child psychopathology. Despite this complexity, the clinician can conduct an assessment in an intentional, systematic, and thoughtful manner. The application of relevant theory (systemic, developmental) and research to case material guides the clinician's decisions about what *method* to use to gather *what type* of information from *whom*. A client-centered perspective facilitates an assessment process that is respectful and collaborative, with results that are meaningful to the family.

As can be seen from the case illustration, a CFP assessment overlaps somewhat with typical assessment practice in an outpatient child behavioral health (BH) clinic. Both types of assessment utilize clinical interviews with children and parents, standardized assessment instruments, information gathering from teachers, and observation of parent–child interaction. However, a systemic assessment expands the observational focus beyond the parent–child dyad, and includes more content domains (e.g., interparental conflict, sibling relationship) than typical child assessment. As a result, a CFP assessment often requires more time (e.g., longer sessions or more sessions) than standard assessment practice. In addition, assessment in systemic practice continues throughout the treatment, as the clinician evaluates the child's and family's progress toward achieving treatment goals.

References

Abidin, R. R. (1995). *Parenting stress index manual* (3rd ed.). Odessa, FL: Psychological Assessment Resources.

Achenbach, T. M. (1991). *Manual for the child behavior checklist/4–18 and 1991 profile.* Burlington, VT: Department of Psychiatry, University of Vermont.

American Psychiatric Association. (2013). *Diagnostic and Statistical Manual of Mental Disorders* (DSM-5®). Arlington, VA: American Psychiatric Association.

Bray, J. H. (2009). Couple and family assessment. In J. H. Bray & M. Stanton (Eds.), *The Wiley-Blackwell handbook of family psychology* (pp. 151–164). Oxford: Wiley-Blackwell.

Eyberg, S. M., Chase, R. M., Fernandez, M. A., & Nelson, M. M. (2014). *Dyadic Parent-Child Interaction Coding System (DPICS): Clinical manual* (4th ed.). Gainesville, FL: PCIT International.

Eyberg, S. M., & Pincus, D. (1999). *Eyberg child behavior inventory and Sutter-Eyberg student behavior inventory-revised: Professional manual.* Odessa, FL: Psychological Assessment Resources.

Fincham, F. D., & Linfield, K. J. (1997). A new look at marital quality: Can spouses feel positive and negative about their marriage? *Journal of Family Psychology, 11*(4), 489–502.

Fleuridas, C., Nelson, T. S., & Rosenthal, D. M. (1986). The evolution of circular questions: Training family therapists. *Journal of Marital and Family Therapy, 12*(2), 113–127.

Grotevant, H. D., & Carlson, C. I. (1989). *Family assessment: A guide to methods and measures.* New York, NY: Guilford Press.

Hamilton, E., & Carr, A. (2016). Systematic review of self-report family assessment measures. *Family Process, 55*(1), 16–30.

Hampson, R. B., & Beavers, W. R. (2004). Observational assessment of couples and families. In L. Sperry (Ed.), *Assessment of couples and families: Contemporary and cutting-edge strategies* (pp. 91–115). New York, NY: Brunner-Routledge.

March, J. S. (2000). *Manual for the multidimensional anxiety scale for children* (2nd ed.). Toronto: Multi-Health Systems.

McGoldrick, M., Gerson, R., & Petry, S. S. (2008). *Genograms: Assessment and intervention* (3rd ed.). New York, NY: WW Norton & Company.

McNeil, C. B., & Hembree-Kigin, T. L. (2011). *Parent—child Interaction therapy* (2nd Ed.). New York, NY: Springer Science & Business Media.

Reynolds, C. R., & Kamphaus, R. W. (2015). *Behavior assessment system for children—3rd edition (BASC-3).* New York, NY: Pearson Assessments.

Stanton, M., & Welsh, R. K. (2011). *Specialty competencies in couple and family psychology.* Oxford: Oxford University Press.

Tomm, K. (1987). Interventive interviewing: Part I. Strategizing as a fourth guidelinfor the therapist. *Family Process, 26*(1), 3–13.

CHAPTER 4

Evidence-Based Practice and Treatment Planning

In developing a treatment plan, a clinician integrates the case formulation with available research on relevant empirically supported interventions and information about the family's beliefs and values. This process drives the clinician's and caregivers' collaborative decisions about the selection and sequencing of interventions. Efforts to integrate science and clinical data in treatment planning are consistent with the movement toward evidence-based practice (EBP) embraced by medicine and health service psychology, and can be defined as "the integration of the best available research with clinical expertise in the context of patient characteristics, culture, and preferences" (APA Presidential Task Force on Evidence-Based Practice, 2006, p. 273). The following section briefly describes evidence-based interventions for the Medina family problems identified during the assessment phase. These problems include child anxiety, school refusal, disruptive behavior, and couple distress. Next, a model is presented for selecting and organizing these interventions within a systemic and integrative framework. Finally, a collaborative model for treatment planning is presented and illustrated with the Medina family.

Evidence-Based Interventions

Several systems have been proposed to categorize the level of research support for a psychological treatment. According to the system used to classify treatments for children (Southam-Gerow & Prinstein, 2014), *well-established treatments* have the highest level of empirical support, followed by *probably efficacious treatments* and then *possibly efficacious treatments*. A *well-established treatment* has been tested in at least two large-scale randomized controlled trials that have demonstrated its superior efficacy to some other treatment (e.g., a placebo or another treatment); these trials must have been conducted by independent teams working in different research settings. A *probably efficacious treatment* meets the standard of two trials, but has not yet met the independent investigator criterion. A *possibly efficacious (or "promising") treatment* may have one strong trial showing that it is better than no treatment, or a number of smaller clinical studies without all of the appropriate methodological controls.

Within couple and family psychology (CFP), interventions can be classified according to three levels, providing a hierarchical index of confidence of treatment efficacy: (a) evidence-informed interventions, (b) promising interventions, (c) evidence-based treatments (Sexton et al., 2011). There are many interventions that meet the criteria for evidence-based treatments in CFP. These interventions typically integrate two or more systemic theoretical approaches into a unifying conceptual framework (*model*) and target a specific problem and population (e.g., adolescents with substance abuse). However, most of these model-based approaches address the problems of couples or adolescents rather than children under 12 years.

Anxiety Disorders

Decades of research and a number of reviews have established cognitive behavioral therapy (CBT) as the most effective and appropriate first-line treatment for children with anxiety disorders. Initial reviews (e.g., Silverman, Pina, & Viswesvaran, 2008) examined comprehensive, *name brand* CBT programs with treatment manuals. Subsequent reviews (Chorpita et al., 2011; Higa-McMillan et al., 2016) evaluated broader categories of treatments with common therapeutic elements (i.e., individual protocols that each involve self-monitoring, coping, and associated behavioral exercises). These reviews found that a number of CBT treatments demonstrated the best support (i.e., *well-established treatments*) based on statistically significant symptom reduction in randomized clinical trials. Another way to evaluate a treatment is to assess its impact on functional impairment, that is, whether it is responsible for clinically significant change in the child's daily life. According to this more demanding standard, CBT (treatment including cognitive management techniques, with or without exposure) met the criteria for a *well-established treatment*, and CBT with parents, CBT with medication, and exposure met criteria for a *probably efficacious treatment* (Higa-McMillan et al., 2016).

Recent reviews have noted the frequency of various practice elements among the most efficacious treatments. A practice element is a discrete clinical technique or strategy (e.g., relaxation) used as part of a larger intervention plan (Chorpita, Daleiden, & Weisz, 2005). The identification of effective practice elements is especially useful for clinicians who do not have access to or competence in providing name brand CBT treatment packages. According to the Higa-McMillan et al. (2016) review, exposure was the most commonly occurring practice element derived from *well-established treatments*, employed in 88 percent of study conditions. Cognitive techniques were the second-most commonly occurring practice element, followed by relaxation, psychoeducation for the child, and modeling.

As the evidence base for CBT has grown, researchers have explored the question: for whom does CBT work best and in what context? Children least likely to benefit from CBT include those from families with lower socioeconomic status, those with more severe baseline psychopathology, or those whose parents experience more psychopathology and caregiver stress (Wergeland et al., 2016). Conversely, these data suggest that CBT *not* involving parents is best conducted with children with mild to moderate anxiety and parents without psychopathology, from middle- to high-income families with few stressors.

Given the documented role of parenting behavior in the maintenance of child anxiety, many CBT programs include parents in a deliberate and systematic way. Some CBT treatments involve the parent as a coach or co-therapist, supporting the child's mastery of coping skills. Other interventions, sometimes called family-focused CBT, conceptualize the parent as a co-client, and explicitly address parenting behavior or parent anxiety management. Sessions are held separately or conjointly with the parent and child, and parents participate in some or all of the child's sessions. Randomized controlled trials comparing individual CBT to CBT involving the parent have yielded mixed results, in part due to the different ways in which the parent's role in treatment has been defined. There is some evidence that family-focused CBT outperforms individual CBT when it targets parental intrusiveness (e.g., Wood et al., 2009). However, intrusiveness is not the only parent behavior contributing to child anxiety; parenting stress, family conflict, and tension in the couple relationship also may be important. Family-focused CBT may prove more efficacious than individual CBT when it targets the specific family processes and parenting behaviors that maintain the child's anxiety in a given family. However, this type of intervention requires a systemic case conceptualization and skills in family therapy, which are outside the skillset of many clinicians trained in CBT.

School Refusal

School refusal, defined as refusal to go to school or persistent difficulty in remaining in class for the entire school day, is not a psychiatric diagnosis. The most common primary diagnoses associated with school refusal among five to 17-year olds are separation anxiety disorder, generalized anxiety disorder, and oppositional defiant disorder, though nearly a third of youth with this problem do not meet criteria for any psychiatric diagnosis (Kearney & Albano, 2004). Children tend to refuse school for one or more of four reasons, namely to: (a) stay away from situations that make them uncomfortable or distressed, (b) avoid social or evaluative situations perceived as painful, (c) receive attention from a parent, or (d) obtain tangible rewards outside of school (Kearney & Albano, 2004). Thus, school refusal behavior is negatively reinforced by avoidance of unpleasant situations, positively reinforced by rewards or parental attention, or both. According to this model, children who refuse school to avoid negative affect benefit from CBT that includes psychoeducation, exercises to control somatic symptoms and reduce distress, cognitive restructuring, and progressive exposure to school situations perceived as stressful. Children who avoid school to seek parental attention or rewards profit from family therapy targeting the establishment of education-related routines and contingency management (e.g., positive consequences for school attendance). Returning the child to school as soon as possible is a priority for both types of treatment. Accordingly, therapy sessions are frequent, with daily check-ins or attendance journals, and the clinician must be available to respond quickly to emerging obstacles to school attendance. Relapse prevention is also a key part of treatment.

As school refusal does not remit in the absence of treatment (King et al., 1998), standardized CBT protocols have been developed to improve school attendance (e.g., Heyne & Rollings, 2002). CBT for anxiety-based school refusal has been empirically supported by case studies as well as randomized clinical trials. However, children who refuse school for other reasons or who have co-morbid externalizing behavior problems have often been excluded from this research (Kearney, 2008). Only one published trial has tested the merit of parent involvement in CBT for school refusal; interventions including parent training improved school attendance more than child CBT at post-treatment, but not at follow-up (Heyne et al., 2002). Existing treatment manuals do not offer guidelines for selecting and sequencing treatment components to match the appropriate level of parent involvement or to target change in family interaction patterns. Researchers have begun to examine the efficacy of a flexible, formulation-driven CBT approach, in which the interventions and format (child, parent, or family sessions) depend on co-occurring psychopathology and the function of the school refusal behavior (Tolin et al., 2009). Thus, evidence-based practice in cases of school refusal usually consists of comprehensive and intensive interventions that integrate individual CBT strategies with parent training or family therapy, and consultation with physicians (for children's somatic complaints) and teachers.

Disruptive Behavior

The psychological treatment with the strongest evidence for treating disruptive behavior disorders is parent training (also called behavioral family-based intervention), defined as an intervention in which parents actively acquire parenting skills to manage their child's challenging behavior. There are several manualized treatments that meet the criteria for *well-established treatment*, including Parent Management Training—Oregon model (Patterson et al., 1975), Triple P: Positive Parenting Program (Sanders, 1999), Incredible Years program (Webster-Stratton & Hammond, 1997), and Parent–Child Interaction Therapy (PCIT; Brinkmeyer & Eyberg, 2003). All these programs target parents of children under 12 years of age, and require that clinicians receive specialized training and certification in the particular treatment model. Only PCIT requires that the referred child be present during most sessions, as the primary proposed change mechanism is live coaching of the parent in using specific parenting and discipline skills in dyadic interactions with the child. Unfortunately, very few studies have used a systematic cultural adaptation process to test the effectiveness of these evidence-based programs for ethnic minority parents (Baumann et al., 2015).

All evidence-based parenting training programs are grounded in behavioral and attachment theories. Given these common theoretical roots and the financial barriers to training and certification in the manualized treatments, a more *practice-friendly* approach to evidence-based intervention is the identification and evaluation of strategies shared by efficacious programs. In a meta-analysis of parent training programs for children zero to seven years of age, Kaminski et al. (2008) identified 18 program components, of which several were associated with larger effect sizes regardless of other program content or delivery. Two components were reliably associated with more success in both improving parenting behavior and reducing child externalizing behavior problems: training in creating positive interactions with the child, and requiring parents to practice new skills with their own child during sessions. Additional program components reliably associated with reduced child externalizing behaviors were parent training in using time-out as a disciplinary technique and responding consistently to the child's behaviors. Contrary to commonly held beliefs, programs utilizing a manual or curriculum did not demonstrate larger effect sizes than programs without a standardized protocol.

A disadvantage of the *common practice element* approach is that a program component may not be successful if it is applied outside of the conceptual framework within which it was developed. A good example of this is the practice of training parents to use *time-out* as a consequence for noncompliant or disruptive child behavior. Most evidence-based parent training programs teach the time-out procedure only after parents have mastered the skill of building positive interactions with their child; after all, developmental and behavioral theories indicate that *time-out* is not effective if *time-in* (e.g., playing with parent) is not perceived by the child as positive. Therefore, implementing the time-out procedure too early in parent training, and particularly before the child has experienced increases in parental warmth, may be unsuccessful and cause frustration for both the parent and the child.

The focus of evidence-based parent training programs tends to be on dyadic processes in the parent–child relationship, such as the coercive interaction patterns or the parent's inadvertent negative reinforcement of the child's noncompliance. Very few evidence-based parent training programs directly address triadic processes in the family, such as the polarization between parents about how to manage a child's disruptive behavior, or a parent's preferential treatment of a sibling over the target child. Yet, given the data on the *spillover* of marital and family conflict into the parent–child relationship, it is unlikely that families can sustain improvements from parent training if other aspects of the family climate are unfavorable to the child's development. Despite evidence that case complexity does not influence clinical outcome or limit the applicability of evidence-based treatments for disruptive behavior (Kazdin & Whitley, 2006), parent training may be a necessary, but not sufficient, component of a systemic treatment plan for child disruptive behavior.

Couple Distress

Couple distress refers to the level of distress experienced by partners in their relationship with one another, regardless of the reason for the distress. Several types of treatment for couple distress have been developed and tested. Based on the behavioral view that couple distress results from low levels of positive reinforcement paired with high levels of coercive exchange, behavioral couples therapy (BCT) identifies specific behavioral targets for change and salient reinforcers that can be used to facilitate this change. Specific intervention strategies include problem-solving skills training and behavioral contracting, in which the desired behavior of one partner is exchanged for the desired behavior of the other. Integration of cognitive strategies into BCT expands the domain of clinical inquiry to include partners' cognitions and attributions about one another and the relationship. Integrative behavioral couple therapy (IBCT; Christensen & Jacobson, 2000) incorporates attention to the partners' emotional experience, focusing on understanding and changing unhelpful beliefs and destructive behavioral patterns, and on emotional acceptance when behavior change is not possible. Emotion-focused therapy (EFT; Johnson, 2004) is an experiential approach based on attachment as a model for intimate relationships; EFT aims to shape in-session interactions in which partners express attachment needs and fears, and become more emotionally responsive to one another.

Among couple therapies, BCT, IBCT, and EFT have the strongest record of support (Lebow et al., 2012). None of these approaches has been demonstrated to be superior to the others in reducing couple distress. Consequently, some family researchers (Sprenkle, Davis, & Lebow, 2009) focus on common factors found across evidence-based couple therapies, including a systemic perspective and the use of intervention strategies that address emotion, cognition, and behavior. Similarly, Christensen (2010) proposed principles of evidence-based treatment for couple distress: (a) formulating a dyadic case conceptualization, (b) finding constructive ways to cope with emotion, (c) building intimacy by sharing private, emotion-based experience, (d) facilitating productive communication, and (e) emphasizing strengths and positive behavior.

Couple distress is typically an unremitting problem that does not improve without treatment (Lebow et al., 2012), and is often exacerbated by stress and conflict related to parenting. There are no published studies comparing different couple therapy approaches in the context of treatment for a child with behavior problems. In clinical practice, the partners' parenting stress and co-parenting conflict often can be addressed directly with parent training and family therapy. If treatment progress is impeded by couple distress unrelated to parenting, the couple may be referred to another clinician for couple therapy. However, it is possible to integrate the principles of couple therapy into parent training and family therapy, fitting evidence-based strategies to the couple's needs and preferences, based on a systemic formulation of the family processes contributing to the child's behavior problems.

Organization and Selection of Interventions

Case Formulation

For children with emotional and behavior problems, treatment planning is too complex a process to be fully driven by research. Families often present with a number of interrelated problems that could be resolved by several competing strategies, placing the informed clinician in a quandary. How should treatment goals be prioritized? For example, a separated couple with an anxious child might benefit from couple therapy to reduce partners' conflict with one another as well as parent training to diminish parenting behaviors that contribute to the child's anxiety. Given limited resources, which intervention should be recommended first? The answer depends in part on the case formulation. If the conflict between the partners is driving both the suboptimal parenting and the child's anxiety, couple therapy should be prioritized over parent training.

However, the case formulation alone is often insufficient to guide the clinician in selecting from a range of divergent or conflicting therapy approaches, in part because of the complex, reciprocal influences among family processes. For example, the Medina parents' parenting stress, couple distress, and perceived preferential treatment of the brother contribute to Elena's anxiety and oppositional behavior, and Elena's challenging behaviors reciprocally lead to more parenting stress and couple discord, and greater parental distancing from Elena. Should the intervention target Elena's anxiety, the couple's relationship, their parenting, or the relationship each parent has with Elena? Should the intervention be individual CBT for Elena, parent training for the couple, or family therapy? To answer these questions, specific criteria for intervention selection are needed.

Criteria for Selection of Interventions

Historically, case formulation and treatment planning in CFP were guided by different schools of theory rather than by empirical research. However, the field now has a shared base of principles, concepts, strategies, and common factors. Although there exist meta-models that offer algorithms for choosing interventions based on a case formulation (e.g., Pinsof et al., 2011), most clinicians draw on diverse sources to select treatment strategies likely to be successful and with which they feel comfortable (Lebow, 2014).

In selecting an intervention based on a case formulation, the clinician faces two questions. First, *what are the proximate and ultimate goals for treatment?* Second, *what is the most effective, efficient, lasting, developmentally appropriate, acceptable, and accessible method to achieve these goals?* It is important to note that these questions do not view any one level of human experience (e.g., nuclear family) as more important than another (e.g., biological). Although early models of family therapy tended to privilege the family experience over others, an integrative perspective views all levels as important, as change at any one level affects functioning at the other levels (Lebow, 2014). For example, interventions to increase support for parents within their friend and family networks can lead to improved parenting, which can result in a stronger parent–child bond and diminished emotional and behavioral problems for the child.

Efficacy

Parents may request a particular intervention because they believe it will be helpful to their child. However, the preferences of parents or referral sources should not be used to justify an intervention that does not have an evidence base demonstrating its efficacy for the presenting problem. For example, a clinician should not conduct play therapy to reduce a child's oppositional behavior any more than a physician should prescribe an antibiotic for a virus. It is the clinician's responsibility to educate parents about evidence-based interventions. If several evidence-based approaches exist (e.g., IBCT and EFT for couple distress), parent preferences can be used to select among them. If there are no documented evidence-based models or treatment strategies for the presenting problem, the clinician can propose interventions that are consistent with theory and accumulated knowledge about child development and family functioning.

A number of interventions can be considered for the Medina family based on the case formulation and the available evidence for interventions targeting child anxiety, disruptive behavior, school refusal, or couple distress. These interventions include: individual CBT for Elena, CBT with parent, family-focused CBT, parent training for the couple, and couple therapy to reduce marital discord. Within any of these intervention categories (e.g., couple therapy), the clinician can rely on a single evidence-based model (e.g., EFT) or apply integrated concepts and techniques from multiple evidence-based protocols (i.e., common factors or practice elements). Two or more interventions (e.g., individual CBT and parent training) can be offered simultaneously or sequentially, depending on the family's preferences and resources.

Efficiency and Durability

Although research has yielded promising data about the durability of several evidence-based treatment models, estimates about an intervention's efficiency and durability are not based solely on empirical data. Considerations of efficiency focus on the time and human costs of the intervention relative to the expected outcome. For example, a parent training program in which the clinician meets separately with each parent is less efficient than one in which the parents are seen together. Durability refers to the sustainability of changes after the intervention has been completed. For example, targeted changes in disciplinary practices are likely to be sustainable if the parents apply them in session with their child and across multiple situations.

Developmentally Appropriate

The goal of treatment for children with emotional and behavioral problems is to return them to a developmental trajectory in which they are moving toward greater mastery and independence in several different domains simultaneously. Most children between two and 12 years are in the process of developing greater awareness and regulation of their emotions, and more independence from their primary attachment figures. Interventions that buck this trend are not developmentally appropriate. For example, it would be developmentally inappropriate for a clinician to promote or sanction anxiety reduction via co-sleeping of mother and child after the child has already demonstrated independence in sleeping alone. In the case of Elena, a developmentally appropriate treatment target is the school refusal, as children's developmental progression in multiple domains is jeopardized by a significant interruption in formal education. Thus, treatment planning for the Medina family should prioritize Elena's school attendance.

In addition, interventions should be developmentally appropriate in their content, format, and techniques. Depending on the family's culturally influenced values and beliefs, some topics (e.g., sex, money, marital tension) should not be discussed in the presence of children. Treatment techniques and strategies are ideally matched to children's cognitive and emotional abilities. For example, young children should not be expected to participate in discussions of abstract concepts (e.g., trust) without some explanation that defines the concept in terms they can understand. Similarly, interventions that teach negotiation skills may be appropriate for adolescents and their parents, but may not be developmentally appropriate for children.

Acceptability

Interventions known to be effective are unlikely to be successful if they are not acceptable to families. Acceptability refers to the extent to which the family views the intervention content (what is discussed), approach (techniques, stance of therapist), and format (who is present) as appropriate for their needs, values, beliefs, and cultural context. For example, some couples may feel comfortable discussing parenting disagreements in the presence of their children, whereas those invested in showing a *united front* of parental authority may prefer to discuss their conflict without the children present. Similarly, parents may decline a treatment that requires the child's acceptance of a psychiatric diagnosis. Interventions can be adapted or tailored to families' cultural contexts with explicit integration of language, cultural beliefs, and explanatory models compatible with the family's cultural history and experience (Kelly, 2017; also see Chapter 6 for a discussion of cultural diversity). Given the Medina parents' stated goals of improving Elena's school attendance and decreasing her tantrums, the interventions they may deem most acceptable are parent training and CBT targeting school refusal.

Accessibility

Accessibility focuses on the availability of the intervention and the family's resources (insurance, transportation, childcare) to attend treatment sessions. For children raised by more than one caregiver, parent training and family therapy work best when both caregivers can attend sessions. A caregiver's extended absence may make these interventions less accessible. For the Medina family, all of the interventions are assumed to be accessible, but this is often not the case in some communities, where play therapy may be the only intervention available.

Putting It All Together

Treatment planning requires the clinician to consider a number of interventions, simultaneously evaluating their efficacy, efficiency, durability, developmental appropriateness, acceptability, and accessibility. The clinician and family then collaboratively choose one or more interventions over the others. In some cases, the clinician and the family have different preferences; for example, the clinician may prefer weekly parent training for its demonstrated efficacy in reducing child disruptive behavior and improving parent–child relationships. However, the parents may prefer to meet episodically with the clinician for crisis intervention. In this case, the clinician is ethically bound to inform parents that sporadic sessions may help with crisis resolution, but yield little success in improving the child's disruptive behavior.

Table 4.1 illustrates how the interventions considered for the Medina family might meet the aforementioned selection criteria. It is important to note that the table does not include all of the key clinical decisions to be made about Elena's treatment. For example, it excludes consideration of anti-anxiety medication and a clinician-sanctioned home-bound education program. However, these decisions can be evaluated by similar criteria. Implementation of a home-bound education program may efficiently improve Elena's anxiety-driven disruptive behavior, but it does not address her school refusal, as she would continue to be reinforced for avoiding school.

According to Table 4.1, family-focused CBT and parent training appear to meet all six criteria for the Medina family. The next step in treatment planning is to discuss the order, format, and staffing for the interventions.

Collaborative Treatment Planning

The collaborative treatment planning process includes decisions about the selection, sequencing, and format of interventions. Two or more interventions may be implemented simultaneously or sequentially, depending on service availability and family preference. Treatment may progress more quickly if the interventions are offered simultaneously, rather than sequentially.

Table 4.1 *Interventions by selection criteria for the Medina family*

Intervention	Efficacy	Efficiency	Durability	Developmental appropriateness	Acceptability	Accessibility
Individual CBT	X		X	X	X	X
CBT with parent as coach	X			X	X	X
Family-focused CBT	X	X	X	X	X	X
Parent training with couple	X	X	X	X	X	X
Couple therapy	X		X	N/A		X

The format for an intervention may consist of a meeting with the child and one parent, the parents without the child present, two generations of caregivers, the entire family, or some combination of these. Clinicians conducting therapy from a systemic perspective make continual and evolving decisions about session format; who to include in what meetings depends on the case formulation, the specific goals and the family's progress toward goal attainment, and the family's preference. In the case of multiple or changing formats, the clinician must monitor how one format affects the other (see Chapter 6 for a discussion of related ethical issues). For example, if the child is sometimes seen individually and at other times with her family, the clinician should consider the impact of this changing format on the child's honesty in the individual context and on the parents' willingness to trust the clinician to use planned interventions when they are not present (Lebow, 2014).

When two or more interventions are recommended, the clinician and family jointly decide whether the interventions will be provided by the same clinician or different clinicians. When two or more clinicians are involved in the treatment, difficulties between them may arise that parallel the core problems in the family. Active coordination between two therapists providing different interventions is needed to move in sync toward proximate and ultimate treatment goals. The same is true for a clinician providing therapy and a psychiatrist or pediatrician managing a child's medication.

Treatment Formulation

In the treatment formulation, a plan for problem resolution is negotiated with the family. For the Medina family, some form of CBT is recommended. This intervention aims to help Elena identify when she starts to feel anxious or uncomfortable (i.e., before she is at a *10*), and successfully use coping skills to manage her anxiety, with parental support. An additional goal is to develop a plan for regular school attendance that utilizes Elena's coping skills in the school setting, and includes gradual exposure and positive reinforcement for success. An important treatment component will be support of the parents' communication with school staff to coordinate a plan for monitoring Elena's attendance and responding to her requests to see the nurse. Simultaneously, parent training is recommended to change the family processes resulting from and contributing to Elena's challenging behaviors. These processes include the parents' emotional reactions to Elena's defiance, their inconsistent and unpredictable disciplinary practices, the tension in their co-parenting relationship, and their lack of peer and family support.

The clinician shared the case formulation with Karen and Emilio at the end of the third assessment session, providing a simpler overview to the family when the children were present. The formulation was offered as a tentative hypothesis; the clinician asked the parents whether the hypothesis made sense to them, and if they had additional ideas about what might be contributing to Elena's behavior problems. Emilio and Karen discussed other family members who had suffered from anxiety as children, including Karen's younger brother. After a discussion about the available interventions to treat Elena's school refusal, anxiety, and oppositional behavior, the parents selected family-focused CBT to target school refusal and anxiety, and parent sessions to help them work better together to manage Elena's difficult behavior. After a discussion of how treatment would fit into the family's schedule, the parents stated a preference for initial CBT sessions to include Elena and Karen, rather than the whole family. When the clinician asked the parents how Elena would understand Julian's absence from sessions, the parents decided that Julian should attend so that Elena would not feel like "she is the problem." Emilio added that Julian would benefit from learning some of the coping skills taught to his sister, but also stated that Elena may prefer to have some one-on-one time with the clinician to learn the skills before she "teaches" her brother. The clinician and family agreed that some CBT sessions would be held with Elena and others would include the whole family.

Conclusion

Selection and integration of interventions for child emotional and behavioral problems are based on a systemic case conceptualization and consideration of interventions according to their efficacy, efficiency, durability, developmental appropriateness, acceptability, and accessibility. Clinicians may use one or more established, evidence-based intervention models, or they may flexibly incorporate concepts and techniques from multiple evidence-based protocols (i.e., common factors) to change family processes and meet treatment goals. Interventions and techniques are conceptualized and applied systemically, no matter how many individuals are present during treatment sessions. Any intervention can be systemic if it is driven by a systemic case conceptualization and addresses systemic etiological factors.

Treatment planning is a complex, integrative process that evolves over the course of therapy to accommodate the clinician's growing understanding of the case, especially the contextual factors impeding problem resolution. However, treatment planning also changes over the course of a clinician's professional life, as he or she gains additional clinical experience and applies new research findings to practice.

References

APA Presidential Task Force on Evidence-Based Practices. (2006). Evidence-based practice in psychology. *American Psychologist, 61*(4), 271–285.

Baumann, A. A., Powell, B. J., Kohl, P. L., Tabak, R. G., Penalba, V., Proctor, E. K., Domenech-Rodriguez, M. M., & Cabassa, L. J. (2015). Cultural adaptation and implementation of evidence-based parent-training: A systematic review and critique of guiding evidence. *Child Youth Services Review, 53*, 113–120.

Brinkmeyer, M. Y., & Eyberg, S. M. (2003). Parent-child interaction therapy for oppositional children. In A. E. Kazdin & J. R. Weisz (Eds.), *Evidenced-based psychotherapies for children and adolescents* (pp. 204–223). New York, NY: Guilford Press.

Chorpita, B. F., Daleiden, E. L., & Weisz, J. R. (2005). Identifying and selecting the common elements of evidence based interventions: A distillation and matching model. *Mental Health Services Research, 7*(1), 5–20.

Chorpita, B. F., Daleiden, E. L., Ebesutani, C., Young, J., Becker, K. D., Nakamura, B. J., Phillips, L., Ward, A., Lynch, R., Trent, L., Smith, R. L., Okamura, K., & Starace, N. (2011). Evidence based treatments for children and adolescents: An updated review of indicators of efficacy and effectiveness. *Clinical Psychology: Science and Practice, 18*(2), 154–172.

Christensen, A. (2010). A unified protocol for couple therapy. In K. Hahlweg, M. Grawe-Gerber, & D. H. Baucom (Eds.), *Enhancing couples: The shape of couple therapy to come* (pp. 33–46). Cambridge, MA: Hogrefe Publishing.

Christensen, A., & Jacobson, N. S. (2000). *Reconcilable differences*. New York, NY: Guilford Press.

Higa-McMillan, C. K., Francis, S. E., Rith-Najarian, L., & Chorpita, B. F. (2016). Evidence base update: 50 years of research on treatment for child and adolescent anxiety. *Journal of Clinical Child & Adolescent Psychology, 45*(2), 91–113.

Heyne, D., King, N. J., Tonge, B. J., Rollings, S., Young, D., Pritchard, M., & Ollendick, T. H. (2002). Evaluation of child therapy and caregiver training in the treatment of school refusal. *Journal of the American Academy of Child & Adolescent Psychiatry, 41*(6), 687–695.

Heyne, D., & Rollings, S. (2002). *School refusal*. Oxford: Blackwell Scientific Publications.

Johnson, S. M. (2004). *Creating connections: The practice of emotionally focused marital therapy* (2nd ed.). New York, NY: Brunner-Routledge.

Kaminski, J. W., Valle, L. A., Filene, J. H., & Boyle, C. L. (2008). A meta-analytic review of components associated with parent training program effectiveness. *Journal of Abnormal Child Psychology, 36*(4), 567–589.

Kazdin, A. E., & Whitley, M. K. (2006). Comorbidity, case complexity, and effects of evidence-based treatment for children referred for disruptive behavior. *Journal of Consulting and Clinical Psychology, 74*(3), 455–467.

Kearney, C. A. (2008). School absenteeism and school refusal behavior in youth: A contemporary review. *Clinical Psychology Review, 28*(3), 451–471.

Kearney, C. A., & Albano, A. M. (2004). The functional profiles of school refusal behavior: Diagnostic aspects. *Behavior Modification, 28*(1), 147–161.

Kelly, S. (Ed.). (2017). *Diversity in couple and family therapy: Ethnicities, sexualities, and socioeconomics*. Santa Barbara, CA: Praeger/ABC-CLIO, LLC.

King, N. J., Tonge, B. J., Heyne, D., Pritchard, M., Rollings, S., Young, D., Myerson, N., & Ollendick, T. H. (1998). Cognitive-behavioral treatment of school-refusing children: A controlled evaluation. *Journal of the American Academy of Child & Adolescent Psychiatry, 37*(4), 395–403.

Lebow, J. L., Chambers, A. L., Christensen, A., & Johnson, S. M. (2012). Research on the treatment of couple distress. *Journal of Marital and Family Therapy, 38*(1), 145–168.

Lebow, J. (2014). *Couple and family therapy: An integrative map of the territory*. Washington, DC: American Psychological Association Press.

Patterson, G. R., Reid, J. B., Jones, R. R., & Conger, R. E. (1975). *A social learning approach to family intervention: Families with aggressive children* (Vol. 1). Eugene, OR: Castalia Publishing.

Pinsof, W., Breunlin, D. C., Russell, W. P., & Lebow, J. (2011). Integrative problem-centered metaframeworks therapy II: Planning, conversing, and reading feedback. *Family Process, 50*(3), 314–336.

Sanders, M. R. (1999). Triple P-Positive Parenting Program: Towards an empirically validated multilevel parenting and family support strategy for the prevention of behavior and emotional problems in children. *Clinical Child and Family Psychology Review, 2*(2), 71–90.

Sexton, T., Gordon, K. C., Gurman, A., Lebow, J., Holtzworth-Munroe, A., & Johnson, S. (2011). Guidelines for classifying evidence-based treatments in couple and family therapy. *Family Process, 50*(3), 377–392.

Silverman, W. K., Pina, A. A., & Viswesvaran, C. (2008). Evidence-based psychosocial treatments for phobic and anxiety disorders in children and adolescents. *Journal of Clinical Child & Adolescent Psychology, 37*(1), 105–130.

Southam-Gerow, M. A., & Prinstein, M. J. (2014). Evidence base updates: The evolution of the evaluation of psychological treatments for children and adolescents. *Journal of Clinical Child & Adolescent Psychology, 43*(1), 1–6.

Sprenkle, D. H., Davis, S. D., & Lebow, J. L. (2009). *Common factors in couple and family therapy: The overlooked foundation for effective practice.* New York, NY: Guilford Press.

Tolin, D. F., Whiting, S., Maltby, N., Diefenbach, G. J., Lothstein, M. A., Catalano, A., & Gray, K. (2009). Intensive (daily) behavior therapy for school refusal: A multiple baseline case series. *Cognitive and Behavioral Practice, 16*(3), 332–344.

Webster-Stratton, C., & Hammond, M. (1997). Treating children with early-onset conduct problems: A comparison of child and parent training interventions. *Journal of Consulting and Clinical Psychology, 65*(1), 93–109.

Wergeland, G. J. H., Fjermestad, K. W., Marin, C. E., Bjelland, I., Haugland, B. S. M., Silverman, W. K., Öst, L.-G., Bjaastad, J. F., Oeding, K., Havik, O. E., & Heiervang, E. R. (2016). Predictors of treatment outcome in an effectiveness trial of cognitive behavioral therapy for children with anxiety disorders. *Behaviour Research and Therapy, 76*, 1–12.

Wood, J. J., McLeod, B. D., Piacentini, J. C., & Sigman, M. (2009). One-year follow-up of family versus child CBT for anxiety disorders: Exploring the roles of child age and parental intrusiveness. *Child Psychiatry and Human Development, 40*(2), 301–316.

CHAPTER 5

Systemic Interventions

CFP interventions draw on a shared base of concepts, strategies, and techniques. Many of these concepts and strategies have been explicitly incorporated into an evidence-based treatment model; most are considered *common factors* of evidence-based systemic practice. They can be conceptualized as essential components of the intervention competency in CFP (Celano, Smith, & Kaslow, 2010). For families of children under 12 years, these essential components include: (a) forging and maintaining a systemic therapeutic alliance; (b) building family cohesion and communication; (c) managing negative interactions; (d) improving parenting or family organization; and (e) psychoeducation about relational life, child development, and the etiology of emotional and behavior problems in children. The specific techniques used by the clinician depend on the systemic case conceptualization, the evidence-based intervention model within which the technique is embedded, the family's progress toward treatment goals, and developmental and cultural considerations.

This chapter describes the essential components of the CFP intervention competency in clinical work with children and their families, and demonstrates how clinicians can use CFP intervention knowledge and skills to treat the Medina family's presenting problems. The chapter also discusses how clinicians may collaborate successfully with systems of care and monitor treatment progress.

Incorporating Essential Components into Treatment

Of the five essential components comprising the intervention competency, development of a systemic therapeutic alliance is most important during the initial phase of treatment, as it engages the family in the work of therapy and builds a foundation for the systemic interventions to follow. In practice, all five essential components are integrated throughout treatment, with the priority of any one component at a given time dictated by the systemic formulation and the family's progress toward treatment goals. Although the components are described separately, there is overlap in practice; for example, cohesion-building strategies can be used to strengthen the systemic alliance.

Systemic Therapeutic Alliance

A systemic therapeutic alliance is the quality and strength of the collaborative relationship between family members and clinician, and includes a shared commitment to the goals of therapy in the context of a positive emotional bond (Friedlander, Escudero, & Heatherington, 2006). The therapeutic alliance is more complex in systemic treatment than in individual therapy because: (a) it encompasses relationships between the clinician and each family member, its subsystems (e.g., siblings, parents), and the family as a whole; (b) it is reciprocally influenced by relationships within the family and within the treatment team; and (c) family members present with differing temperaments, motives, developmental and clinical needs, culturally influenced values and beliefs, and perspectives on the problem. An additional complication arises when children under 12 years are included in sessions, as they cannot give informed consent for treatment, and may be unwilling or reluctant participants in the intervention.

Forging a systemic alliance becomes more challenging when one or more family members denies or minimizes the presenting problem, or disagrees with others about its cause or proposed solution. Although there are a few situations in which the clinician should side with one or more family members (e.g., ethical issues such as child abuse), in practice clinicians strive for a balanced stance in which all family members feel safe in therapy, have a shared sense of purpose, and all of their perspectives are equally understood and valued. A systemic perspective ensures that the clinician will not view only one person in the family as vulnerable or in pain, or collude with the child against the parents or vice versa. The therapist's emotional bond must be strong with all members, not just with those who come to every session or speak the most.

Even in the absence of family conflict, a systemic therapeutic alliance may be difficult to develop, given the power differential between adults and children, as well as the tendency for many clinicians to rely on verbal discourse to connect with clients. To build a strong emotional connection with children and engage them in treatment, clinicians need to adjust the rhythm, content, and duration of conversation to the child's developmental level. For example, the clinician may use short sentences and demonstrate points with actions or props. The clinician should use an office that is *child-friendly* (i.e., with toys and without expensive, breakable objects), include siblings in the session, and remain receptive to children's nonverbal and metaphorical communication without insisting on an explanation (Rober, 1998).

Young children often prefer to express themselves and connect with others through play, movement, art, or humor. Play interventions can be useful in engaging both children and parents in treatment (Sori, 2012), but they should be applied in an intentional manner designed to foster a strong emotional bond among family members or between the family and the clinician. Used appropriately, humor can also level the playing field between adults and children, strengthening children's voices in an enterprise they may view as adult-driven.

Some children are pleasantly attention-seeking from the clinician during sessions. It is easy to fall into the trap of attending to a charming child to the exclusion of a withdrawn child or even the parents, inadvertently unbalancing the systemic alliance. All interactions, including nonverbal ones, between the clinician and one or more family members affect the developing systemic alliance.

Evidence-based strategies for developing a therapeutic alliance differ according to the treatment model, presenting problem, and developmental needs of family members. Common strategies include: *joining* behaviors (e.g., validation of feelings), consensus-building related to treatment goals, rekindling commitments to the relationship(s), diffusing hostile exchanges, minimizing blaming attributions, reframing presenting problems in relational terms, and promoting a relational or systemic view of the problem behavior. Humor is a powerful joining mechanism in family therapy, as it can reduce tension, facilitate understanding and connection, and expose similarities and differences among family members in a playful, acceptable manner.

However, the most important ingredient of a systemic alliance is the emotional bond between the clinician and the family members. The clinician facilitates this bond by maintaining respect and appreciation for clients as fellow human beings, with strengths as well as struggles (Madsen, 1999), and by demonstrating empathy for family members' experiences. Empathy is communicated directly during sessions (e.g., sharing concern, frustration or grief), as well as indirectly by remembering important facts about the family or their situation from one session to the next, and maintaining a nonjudgmental attitude (e.g., normalizing parenting mistakes). Clinicians should avoid shaming or humiliating family members when challenging or confronting their behavior or when reviewing their completion of assigned homework (Friedlander, Escudero, & Heatherington, 2006).

Building Cohesion

All evidence-based CFP interventions include techniques designed to enhance family interactions so that members feel a greater sense of belonging and have more positive understanding of and communication with each other. Building cohesion and communication is especially important for children, as they rely on their parents for support, guidance, and protection. Parents need to feel supported and understood by one another, particularly when facing the stress of child illness or psychopathology. Parents also want and expect a strong, positive relationship with their child in the elementary school years, before the *storm* and turmoil of adolescence sets in.

Without an explicit focus on building or restoring family cohesion, therapy for children may inadvertently contribute to distance or tension in the parent–child relationship. For example, individual cognitive behavioral therapy (CBT) can be successful in reducing a child's anxiety, with downstream positive effects on the parent–child relationship; however, it is important to consider the experience of the parent in the waiting room. Excluded from most (if not all) of the session, the parent may feel cut off from the child's emotional experience and unimportant to the helping process.

If parents are to help children solve their problems, they need to be part of the problem-solving process in therapy. This process usually involves understanding and validating the child's feelings and thoughts, facilitated in therapy by the clinician. However, there are times when a parent is too overwhelmed or emotionally reactive to respond appropriately to the child in a family session, even with the clinician's help. In these situations, the clinician can work individually with the parent to understand and reduce barriers (intrapersonal, relational, developmental, clinical) to appropriate parental responses; when the parent is deemed ready, a conjoint or family session can be implemented with the child present.

Clinicians can also build family cohesion without directly addressing the presenting problem. For example, the clinician may engage the family in a game or ask them to share a positive shared experience (e.g., how they selected their pet) or their perceptions of family strengths. Play interventions are especially useful in building cohesion in families with children (Sori, 2012), given the following caveats. First, the clinician should not attempt a play intervention or discussion of family strengths in the context of high levels of conflict, as family members are likely to decline or sabotage the activity, using it as a vehicle to express anger or disapproval. Second, the play intervention should be developmentally and culturally appropriate for all family members, without privileging any one member or subsystem over others. For example, children participating in a ball toss game should aim from a closer distance to the target than their parents. Third, clinical decisions about the nature, timing, and duration of the play intervention should be based on the systemic formulation, the family's needs and progress, and their observed interaction patterns. Play interventions should be intentional, goal-directed, and clinician-driven, not a *default* activity in therapy.

Following feedback and clarification of treatment goals, the clinician suggested an activity designed to help the parents understand what school is like for Elena and Julian. She asked Elena to play the role of the teacher to her brother (as student), demonstrating what school is like for her on "bad days" and then on "good days." Elena was given paper, a red pen, and pencils, and Julian was told that he had to pretend that his sister was the teacher. Elena gave her brother a spelling test, using words that she had recently learned to spell in her 4th grade class. When Julian said he could not write the words, she told him to do his best. Afterward, she crossed out all of his words with the red pen, and carefully described his mistakes in a voice that oozed with disappointment. She announced to the "class" that anyone who passed the spelling test could get computer time, but Julian had to write the spelling words again. When Elena was asked to demonstrate a good day, she dramatically swept away the paper and pencil from Julian's "desk," exclaiming: "Get ready for pizza, it's Fabulous Friday!" After this demonstration, Elena and Julian switched roles. Julian started to give student Elena some spelling words to write, but Elena interrupted to object to her brother's characterization of the class: "That's not how it is in first grade. All they do is play!"

After the demonstration, the clinician led the family in a discussion about the challenges of school. Elena admitted she worried about doing badly on tests and felt embarrassed when her classmates earned computer time before she did. The clinician asked the parents to recall if they ever felt this way as children, and how they handled these feelings. Both parents remembered disappointments in their own childhood scholastic performance, and suggested that they help Elena study more for spelling tests. The clinician re-directed the discussion to how the parents might help Elena in the moment of "getting it wrong" at school, given that all learning involves making mistakes. Emilio suggested that Elena remind herself of all the times she's done well in school, and Karen offered the phrase: "I have to make mistakes to succeed." The clinician asked the family to think of a time when both kids had to make mistakes in order to learn a motor task, and Julian asked: "like riding my bike?" This comment led to the family's recollection of how many times Elena fell when learning to ride a bike, which she now does quite well. For homework, the clinician asked the parents to make or do something tangible that could help both children remember to put mistakes in perspective while they are at school.

Managing Negative Interactions

Negative interactions are those in which family members express contempt, criticism, sarcasm, rejection, hostility or aggression toward one another, or interact with one another in an overly intrusive, controlling, anxious, or punitive manner. These interactions may occur between any two family members, or across all family relationships. Often, the negative interaction escalates within a dyad (e.g., the mother–son relationship) or *spreads* across the family; for example, a parent yells at the referred child, who in turn pinches a younger sibling.

Managing negative interactions means taking active steps in the session to help family members to stop, reduce, or control the interactions, or prevent their escalation.

It is important for the clinician to manage negative interactions as soon as they occur in the session. When the clinician prevents the conflict from escalating or succeeds in helping family members to express their needs or feelings without criticism or rejection, the family develops more confidence and hope in the intervention, strengthening the systemic therapeutic alliance.

It is neither advisable nor practical to *prevent* family conflict, as family members need to be able to voice disagreement, and they may not know how to disagree without expressing hostility or rejection. In addition, hostile or coercive exchanges can be instructive, as they often drive symptom presentation in the child. For example, a clinician might point out that when the parents raise their voices in anger at each other, the referred child withdraws and clutches her belly. The goal in managing negative interactions is to mine them for information while minimizing their sting. In practice, this means that the clinician needs to be able to both tolerate and appropriately intervene in negative interactions when they occur in session.

There are many ways of intervening to manage negative interactions. An active, *take charge* stance is usually ideal. After acknowledging the disagreement (e.g., "you disagree about the best way to respond to your child's behavior") and validating the perspective of each family member, the clinician can: (a) ask each party to express his or her view directly to the clinician rather than to one another; (b) attempt to negotiate a compromise or foster family members' understanding of both views; or (c) reframe the conflict in relational terms, building consensus about goals. Consider the case of a mother who accuses her daughter of sneaking time on her tablet and lying about it, which the daughter denies in a loud and disrespectful tone, complaining "you're always in a bad mood!" The clinician could reframe the argument: "it sounds like you [mother] want to be able to trust your daughter more, and you [daughter] would like to see your mother in a better mood; both of you want a better relationship with each other."

In some cases, the clinician will manage the conflict by tabling it. For example, if parents argue with one another during a family session about child discipline, the clinician may suggest deferring the discussion to a later time when the child is not present. It is sometimes necessary to directly interrupt a negative interaction without explanation. For example, in the case of sibling squabbling, the clinician can firmly but politely direct the children to attend to the task at hand, rather than to their argument. Alternatively, the clinician can strategically sit between siblings to prevent escalation of aggression. However, these actions should be undertaken only after the parents have had a chance to intervene, and preferably after a systemic therapeutic alliance has been established. Otherwise, parents may feel embarrassed about their powerlessness to manage the children's aggression, and angry that the clinician has temporarily usurped parental authority.

Improving Parenting or Family Organization

Parenting or behavioral management interventions aim to reduce children's behavior problems primarily by teaching parents to: (a) use positive reinforcement for desired behaviors, (b) respond to mild negative behaviors by ignoring them or removing positive reinforcement, (c) implement consistent and predictable consequences for serious negative behavior, and (d) remain calm when disciplining their children. Although children do not have to be present, parenting interventions are more successful if parents can demonstrate the targeted skills with their own child in session (Kaminski et al., 2008). In addition, children may be more motivated to change if they have been included in the discussion about desired positive behaviors and associated rewards, identification of rules, and consequences for breaking the rules.

Interventions to improve family organization generally focus on clarifying or increasing routines, or strengthening boundaries between parents and children, or between the family and the neighborhood, such that family life becomes more safe and predictable. As with parenting training, children are not required to be present at all sessions; however, some sessions should include all family members so that the clinician can observe family interactions, assess whether progress has been made, and if not, intervene accordingly.

Interventions to improve parenting and family organization can target the content of discussions, observed family processes, or both. Consider the case of an anxious eight-year-old boy who voluntarily keeps his bed made and his toys organized in his room while his 13- and 15-year-old brothers make a mess, eat whatever and whenever they want, and come and go as they please. The mother, a single working parent, is out at unpredictable times, often without telling the children when she will return. Initially, the clinician might work with the mother individually to recognize and bolster her leadership role within the family. The goal of these sessions might be to promote safety at home, and to help the mother establish specific routines for communicating with the children about her absences, and who is *in charge* or available to parent when she is out. Then the clinician might meet with the family to assess how the new routines are working, and what additional changes are needed to help everyone feel safe at home.

A more process-oriented intervention addresses the interactions between parents and children as they unfold during the session. For example, consider the case of a seven-year-old girl who casually calls her mother *cray cray*, while her five-year-old twin brothers jump on the furniture, ignoring the mother's repeated requests to sit still. The clinician can strengthen boundaries between parent and children, simultaneously supporting parent authority, in a number of ways. Instructing all the children to sit still might be effective, but is unlikely to succeed for long, and carries the risk of embarrassing the mother by simultaneously highlighting both the children's negative behavior and her helplessness to control it. An alternative approach is to engage the seven-year old in a nonjudgmental exploration of what she meant by *cray cray*, and whether she thinks her mother likes or dislikes this name and why, eliciting the mother's feedback in a nonblaming way. Then, the clinician can introduce an activity that does not require the children to sit still, enlisting the support of the mother as a co-leader.

Emilio and Karen presented to the first "parents only" session in good spirits. Karen reported that she had made both children a bracelet to help them remember that it is okay to make mistakes. Elena had appreciated the bracelet, and was "nice" to both parents for a day or two, but still refused to go to school the next day. The parents noted that Elena tends to miss school on Mondays, Tuesdays, and Wednesdays, but usually attends Thursdays and Fridays, which are Karen's work days. Karen drives the children to school as Emilio has to leave early in the morning to get to work. When asked if there had ever been an exception to this routine, Karen said Emilio took the children to school every day for a week when she was away at a conference a month ago, and Elena did not miss school or complain of stomach pain at all. Emilio smiled at the clinician conspiratorially, saying: "she knew I wouldn't fall for it!" Unsmiling, the clinician looked at both spouses as she pointed out that departures from routine sometimes hold clues for how to solve the problem; her verbal and nonverbal behavior maintained the systemic alliance despite Emilio's subtle bid for approval. Karen playfully offered to go to conferences every week. Emilio said that the family would barely break even, given childcare costs, if Karen worked full time. However, he was not opposed to her adding another shift, and Karen offered to exchange her Friday shift for another day, "since Elena rarely misses fabulous Fridays." The clinician praised the couple for working together to take steps to solve the problem.

Based on the formulation that Elena's school avoidance is due in part to anxiety about the marital tension, the clinician asked Karen and Emilio what they could do on the weekends to help their daughter to worry less on Monday mornings when she has to return to school. The couple agreed that they could spend more fun time together as a family, instead of each parent taking a child to an activity, as they had been doing. The clinician then led a discussion about how the parents should respond when Elena refuses to go to school, suggesting that they come up with a plan that is "scientifically based" (i.e., reinforcing only desired behaviors) but also "consistent, realistic, and fair to both of you." Together they negotiated a plan in which: (a) Emilio awakens Elena and makes sure she gets dressed each morning, while Karen helps Julian and prepares breakfast; (b) parents assume Elena will go to school (e.g., make sure she has her backpack in the car); and (c) Elena is prohibited from using her tablet on the days she misses school. To prevent escalation of conflict in the morning, parents were advised to remind Elena of the consequences of missing school no more than once per day, and to remain calm when Elena refuses to get out of the car. In addition, they agreed on a weekly reward for sustained attendance, starting with a benchmark of three days per week, and working up to five days.

Psychoeducation

Psychoeducation refers to the process of providing information and support to individuals receiving behavioral health (BH) services, and their loved ones, to help them cope with psychiatric disorders in an optimal way. The term has gained traction over the last several decades in concert with advocacy efforts to increase mental health awareness and reduce stigmatization of psychiatric illness. Psychoeducation is different from psychotherapy in that it is often administered in a group setting, is not necessarily assessment-driven, and generally focuses on topics and tools that can be helpful to many families living with psychiatric illness, rather than on problems specific to one family based on an assessment and case formulation. There is no assumption in psychoeducation that family dysfunction causes psychiatric symptoms, but the family is considered crucial to the patient's recovery. Psychoeducation has been incorporated into several evidence-based interventions for children, and multifamily psychoeducation programs have been implemented successfully with children with mood disorders (Fristad et al., 2009).

Psychoeducation in CFP includes relationship education, defined as the provision of knowledge and skills designed to help individuals develop and maintain healthy couple, co-parenting, sibling, and parent–child relationships, or make satisfactory relational adjustments to developmental challenges and transitions. Evidence-based relationship education models have well-defined goals, session structure, and teaching techniques (Ragan et al., 2009). However, psychoeducation also can be integrated into family interventions informally. For example, clinicians may provide family members with information about relational life, child development, or the etiology of childhood emotional and behavior problems. In the Medina case, the clinician can educate the parents about how anxiety in children often *masquerades* as irritability and tantrums. In addition, the clinician could point out how parents often become polarized in perceptions of their child's negative behavior and approaches to behavioral management, as well as certain steps they can take to prevent or minimize this polarization.

Interdisciplinary Collaboration

Interdisciplinary collaboration is an important part of systemic BH service delivery for children. Consistent with the foundational competencies of relationships and professional values and attitudes (Celano, in press), the functional competency of interdisciplinary or interprofessional systems specifies that CFP specialists are knowledgeable about and apply core competencies for interprofessional practice (Interprofessional Education Collaborative Expert Panel, 2011). Interprofessional practice competencies describe specific skills (e.g., shared decision-making) required for teamwork and effective interdisciplinary functioning in health-care settings.

For children, a partner in BH care is the school system. Effective interdisciplinary collaboration between BH professionals and the school system is important because: (a) behavior problems in the classroom can interfere with optimal educational outcomes for all of the students present; (b) the teacher's classroom management or instructional techniques may be a poor match for a given child's needs or contribute to the symptoms; (c) interactions between parents and school staff can help or hinder the child's achievement and classroom behavior; and (d) communication among the parents, the clinician, and school staff is needed to identify the child's education needs, remedy problems, and monitor progress.

Some parents already have soured relationships with the school system by the time they seek BH services. Parents' negative interactions with or perceptions of the school can have an adverse impact on the child. Clinicians should explore the reasons for the parents' dissatisfaction with the school without the child present, and help them improve their relationships with school personnel if doing so serves the best interests of the child. This effort may involve: (a) helping parents understand the organizational culture of the school, including procedures for determining special education eligibility; (b) obtaining information from school staff about their observations of and interactions with the child; or (c) facilitating a meeting between parents and school staff to negotiate a plan for addressing the child's needs or negative behavior.

If the parent has given consent, the clinician can speak directly with the teacher to obtain information to guide the intervention. Collaboration with the school is especially important in treating children with school refusal, as the child's experience in the classroom can be a source of anxiety, fueling avoidance behavior. Also, cooperation of school staff often is needed for a gradual exposure intervention to succeed. In the case of the Medina family, gradual exposure was not needed as Elena was attending school at least a few days every week. However, some classroom activities contributed to Elena's anxiety.

Elena's teacher reported that Elena rushes to complete her work so that she can socialize with friends or get on the computer. She would like Elena to enjoy these privileges, but she is concerned that Elena is not adequately prepared for the upcoming standardized tests, given the number of days she has missed. She noted that Elena's math achievement now lags behind that of her peers. When the clinician asked if she had discussed her concerns with the parents, the teacher said she had not wanted to burden the mother "because she seemed so distraught," but she is ready to speak with her now. When asked how children who miss school generally make up the work, the teacher said that school policy discourages teachers from sending work home if the child is ill. The clinician asked the teacher if she would consider sending home the extra work such that Elena would have the same amount of daily classroom work as the other students. The teacher said she would be willing to do this if the parents agreed to supervise Elena's completion of the assignments according to a schedule she would develop. The clinician shared this plan with the parents, who agreed to help Elena at home to catch up on the work she had missed so that she could enjoy the same reinforcing activities at school as her friends. Elena began to experience less anxiety about her academic performance at school and to look forward to peer socializing and computer time, making it easier for her to attend school consistently.

Monitoring Treatment Progress

Assessment in systemic practice continues throughout treatment, as the clinician evaluates progress toward achieving proximate and ultimate treatment goals. The clinician can monitor the child's and family's treatment progress using the assessment tools described in Chapter 3. For children presenting with behavioral and emotional problems, re-administration of baseline self-report and parent-report measures is one method of determining symptom improvement. For proximate goals such as improved family interaction or coping skills, observational assessment and clinical interview techniques are often best. For example, the clinician may observe parent–child interactions that are characterized by respect and warmth, rather than distance or hostility, suggesting progress toward the proximate goal of an improved parent–child relationship. Clinicians can also ask family members directly about their perceptions of progress, as well as their perceptions about the extent to which the interventions are helping or not helping them reach their goals. According to the competency of reflective practice, CFP specialists invite and value feedback from individuals and families about their interventions or in-session interactions, either in a structured format (Pinsof & Chambers, 2009), or informally via discussion (Celano, in press).

Efforts to monitor treatment progress should take into account the relationship between the family and the clinician, the stage of the therapy (beginning, middle, or end), and the multiple contexts in which treatment is embedded. Given the documented relationship between a split or unbalanced alliance and treatment dropout (Robbins et al., 2003), the systemic alliance should be monitored throughout treatment. A split alliance occurs when family members differ strongly in their attitudes toward the therapy or the therapist, particularly in the treatment goals or the emotional bond with the therapist (Pinsof & Catherall, 1986). Split alliances may result when the clinician fails to engage all family members in shared goals in a way that makes them feel safe, but they may also stem from differing (and conflicting) motives within the family for seeking help (Beck, Friedlander, & Escudero, 2006). Some split alliances are overt, such as when a family member expresses anger at the therapist or leaves the session prematurely. Others are more subtle, and it may be difficult for family members and the clinician to accurately perceive the rupture. To prevent split alliances or minimize their negative impact, the clinician must demonstrate strong interpersonal skills (e.g., responsiveness, ability to generate hope), clear communication, empathy, openness, and the ability to understand and relate to the family as a system (Friedlander, Escudero, & Heatherington, 2006). To evaluate the strength of the systemic therapeutic alliance, the clinician can use formal assessment tools, such as the System for Observing Family Therapy Alliances (SOFTA) described by Friedlander and associates (2006), or informal discussion of the extent to which family members feel that the clinician understands their problems and is helping them work *together* to solve them.

If an alliance becomes split or ruptured, the clinician should take active steps to repair the damage to the alliance, though not all ruptured alliances can be restored. For example, if a father leaves the room in anger after the clinician confronts him in the children's presence about his arguments with his wife, continuing the session in his absence may reify the split alliance and make it more difficult for the clinician to connect with him in the future. In this case, the clinician needs to apologize to the father for how the session got *out of hand* before the next scheduled appointment. The clinician should also inquire about the father's experience of the session, including his associated feelings (anger, betrayal, hurt), and demonstrate appreciation for the father's frankness. The clinician should acknowledge his or her role in the rupture and make a commitment to a course of action that will prevent further damage to family relationships and the systemic alliance. The point of this process is to model for the family how to resolve an interpersonal conflict reasonably and without destroying the relationship.

A second consideration in assessing treatment progress is the stage of treatment, as families may make greater progress and experience more hope earlier in treatment than in the later phases of therapy devoted to skill-building or generalization of gains. Finally, the child's and family's progress in treatment may be influenced by broader contextual factors, such as adverse events affecting the family or community (e.g., parental job loss, natural disaster, neighborhood crime), racism, or poverty. Limited treatment progress in this situation may signal a need for advocacy as well as intervention efforts at a broader systems level.

For the Medina family, proximate treatment goals included: (a) Elena's mastery of coping skills to manage anxiety, (b) cooperation between parents in managing Elena's school refusal and tantrums, and (c) an improved mother–daughter relationship. After four sessions (one family session, two parent sessions, and one session with Elena) over three weeks, the clinician assessed treatment progress.

The clinician assessed Elena's mastery of the coping skills taught in the individual session by asking her to demonstrate the skills to her family. During a family session, she was invited to show the deep breathing skills to her parents or teach the skill to her brother; she chose the latter, and did so successfully, receiving praise from her family and the clinician. To assess cooperation between Emilio and Karen in making parenting decisions, the clinician observed their interaction with one another during sessions and asked in a parent session how they were working together to manage Elena's behavior. Greater cooperation between the two was both observed and reported; Karen reported she felt more supported by her husband, but still feels "blamed" by his parents for Elena's poor behavior, which led to a discussion of cultural differences between the spouses in beliefs and attitudes related to childrearing (see Chapter 6). To assess the relationship between Elena and each of her parents, the clinician asked Karen and Emilio about their recent interactions with Elena. Both reported positive interactions with Elena, but Emilio was more enthusiastic in his descriptions than Karen. To assess progress toward ultimate treatment goals, the clinician kept track of Elena's reported school attendance, and re-administered the Eyberg Child Behavior Inventory (ECBI; Eyberg & Pincus, 1999). Elena's school attendance improved from two days per week at baseline to four days per week. ECBI Intensity ratings decreased for Emilio, but remained high for Karen.

Based on these results, the clinician inquired further about Karen's and Emilio's attributions about Elena's oppositional behavior. Emilio said Elena tests the rules because "she's a kid," while Karen shared her fear that Elena is "turning into" her own mother, described as dishonest and manipulative. Karen said that both Elena and her mother feel "the world revolves around them." The clinician invited Karen to share how she coped with her experience of her mother when she was a child; Karen said she "pulled away," and then began to cry as she realized that she does the same with Elena. The clinician praised Karen for her insight, and cued Emilio to provide emotional support to his wife, which he did by putting his arm around her. The discussion then turned to how the two can work together to remember that Elena is a child (a "work in progress") who needs direction and support from her parents to become honest, empathic adults like them.

Monitoring clients' progress is important in all BH interventions, but it is especially important in systemic practice because there are many levels at which the clinician can intervene; failure to resolve the presenting problem at one level may indicate that intervention at another level is needed. In fact, some CFP treatment models specify an algorithm for deciding when to move from one level to the next. For example, the Metaframeworks model of Breunlin and colleagues (1992) proposes five levels of depth; if intervention at the first level—the level of action—does not solve the problem, it is assumed that meaning and emotion are constraining the solution, and intervention at the experiential level is needed. Deeper levels address historical and intrapsychic constraints to problem-solving. Pinsof's (1995) Integrative Problem-Centered Therapy proposes a similar integrative algorithm. These models indicate that: (a) assessment and intervention are inseparable and co-occurring processes and (b) systemic interventions can target any level of human experience.

Conclusion

All systemic interventions with families require the development and maintenance of a strong systemic therapeutic alliance. In addition, they incorporate four other components: building family cohesion, managing negative interactions, improving parenting or family organization, and psychoeducation. The sequencing and priority of these components is dependent on the case conceptualization, the evidence-based intervention model selected, the family's progress and in-session interactions, and developmental and cultural considerations. Therefore, two children with the same diagnosis may receive different systemic interventions.

A key aspect of systemic practice with children is the need to collaborate with systems of care, including the school system, the pediatrician and the statutory child protection system. Interdisciplinary collaboration requires competencies beyond the usual clinical skills taught in professional training programs and honed under supervised practice. Some families present for treatment with ruptured relationships with partnering systems in their child's development; repair of these ruptures can be a treatment target. Finally, regular monitoring of treatment progress is needed to ensure that the techniques, strategies, and concepts used in the intervention are meaningful and helpful to the family. Monitoring of treatment progress allows the clinician to make *mid-course* corrections, to keep treatment developmentally and culturally appropriate, and to determine when treatment should be terminated.

References

Beck, M., Friedlander, M. L., & Escudero, V. (2006). Three perspectives on clients' experiences of the therapeutic alliance: A discovery-oriented investigation. *Journal of Marital and Family Therapy, 32*(3), 355–368.

Breunlin, D. C., Schwartz, R. C., & Kune-Karrer, B. M. (1992). *Metaframeworks: Transcending the models of family therapy.* San Francisco, CA: Jossey-Bass.

Celano, M. P. (in press). Competencies in couple and family psychology for health service psychologists. In B. H. Fiese (Ed.-in-Chief), M. Celano, K. Deater-Deckard, E.N. Jouriles, & M. M. Whisman (Assoc. Eds.). *APA Handbook of Contemporary Family Psychology* (Vol. 3). Washington, DC: American Psychological Association.

Celano, M. P., Smith, C. O., & Kaslow, N. J. (2010). A competency-based approach to couple and family therapy supervision. *Psychotherapy: Theory, Research, Practice, Training, 47*(1), 35–44.

Eyberg, S. M., & Pincus, D. (1999). *Eyberg child behavior inventory and Sutter-Eyberg student behavior inventory-revised: Professional manual.* Odessa, FL: Psychological Assessment Resources.

Friedlander, M. L., Escudero, V., & Heatherington, L. (2006). *Therapeutic alliances in couple and family therapy: An empirically informed guide to practice.* Washington, DC: American Psychological Association.

Fristad, M. A., Verducci, J. S., Walters, K., & Young, M. E. (2009). Impact of multifamily psychoeducational psychotherapy in treating children aged 8 to 12 years with mood disorders. *Archives of General Psychiatry, 66*(9), 1013–1021.

Interprofessional Education Collaborative Expert Panel. (2011). *Core competencies for interprofessional collaborative practice: Report of an expert panel.* Washington, DC: *Interprofessional Education Collaborative.*

Kaminski, J. W., Valle, L. A., Filene, J. H., & Boyle, C. L. (2008). A meta-analytic review of components associated with parent training program effectiveness. *Journal of Abnormal Child Psychology, 36*(4), 567–589.

Madsen, W. C. (1999). *Collaborative therapy with multi-stressed families.* New York, NY: Guilford Press.

Pinsof, W. M. (1995). *Integrative problem-centered therapy: A synthesis of biological, individual, and family therapy.* New York, NY: Basic Books.

Pinsof, W. M., & Catherall, D. R. (1986). The integrative psychotherapy alliance: Family, couple and individual therapy scales. *Journal of Marital and Family Therapy, 12*(2), 137–151.

Pinsof, W. M., & Chambers, A. L. (2009). Empirically informed systemic psychotherapy: Tracking client change and therapist behavior during therapy. In J. H. Bray & M. Stanton (Eds.), *The Wiley-Blackwell handbook of family psychology* (pp. 431–446). Oxford: Wiley-Blackwell.

Ragan, E. P., Einhorn, L. A., Rhoades, G. K., Markman, H. J., & Stanley, S. M. (2009). Relationship education programs: Current trends and future directions. In J. H. Bray & M. Stanton (Eds.), *The Wiley-Blackwell handbook of family psychology* (pp. 450–462). Oxford: Wiley-Blackwell.

Rober, P. (1998). Reflections on ways to create a safe therapeutic culture for children in family therapy. *Family Process, 37*(2), 201–213.

Robbins, M. S., Turner, C. W., Alexander, J. F., & Perez, G. A. (2003). Alliance and dropout in family therapy for adolescents with behavior problems: Individual and systemic effects. *Journal of Family Psychology, 17*(4), 534–544.

Sori, C. F. (Ed.). (2012). *Engaging children in family therapy: Creative approaches to integrating theory and research in clinical practice.* New York, NY: Routledge.

CHAPTER 6

Foundational Competencies and Termination

Systemic practice is influenced not only by the assessment and intervention competencies described in previous chapters, but also by the foundational competencies that apply to all of the CFP specialist's professional activities. The following sections discuss the individual and cultural diversity (ICD) and ethical and legal foundational competencies, applying them to the Medina case. Special issues associated with termination of systemic treatment also are presented and illustrated with case material. Finally, the foundational competency of reflective practice is discussed as it relates to systemic practice with children and families.

ICD Competency

The ICD competency benchmark for behavioral health (BH) professionals comprises a set of knowledge, skills, and attitudes (awareness and sensitivity) that promotes optimal access to appropriate BH services and favorable clinical processes and outcomes for culturally diverse individuals. Modern conceptualizations of cultural diversity consider this term in its broadest form, incorporating contextual factors and intersectionality among reference group identities that include culture, language, gender, race, ethnicity, ability status, sexual orientation, age, gender identity, socioeconomic status, religion, spirituality, immigration status, education, and employment (American Psychological Association, 2017). Within CFP, the cultural diversity competency includes knowledge of: (a) how self is shaped by ICD factors; (b) the range of reciprocally determined individual, interpersonal, and macrosystemic factors that shape the experience of individuals, couples, families, and organizations; and (c) theory and empirical literature relevant to providing CFP clinical services to multicultural populations (Stanton & Welsh, 2011).

CFP specialists also develop *awareness* of how they have been shaped by ICD factors, including how their own individual, interpersonal, and contextual characteristics shape their perceptions of others (Stanton & Welsh, 2011). For example, a clinician raised by upper middle-class parents in a suburban community unaffected by crime may have difficulty understanding the parenting behavior of low-income caregivers raising children in an urban, crime-affected neighborhood. The clinician could misperceive a mother's strict rules and swift corporal punishment as unnecessarily harsh, rather than as protective measures intended to ensure immediate compliance and safety in an environment perceived as threatening.

The skill component of the ICD competency encompasses alliance development and repair, consideration of contextual factors in assessment and treatment planning, and culturally competent interventions (Stanton & Welsh, 2011). Culturally competent CFP interventions build bridges across differences among the clinician and family members related to four overlapping mechanisms: (a) world views, such as those derived from religion or cultural values; (b) experiences and contexts, such as the context of oppression; (c) power, such as marginalization due to racism or sexism; and (d) the felt distance among people in the therapy session due to the first three differences, such as family members' disengagement or clinician perceptions of helplessness (Kelly, 2017). Skills that promote culturally competent interventions include the use and timing of a genogram to explore cultural identities and practices, linking families to positive community supports, labeling diversity-related differences and helping family members to negotiate them, educating about and normalizing of responses to oppression, recognizing and utilizing strengths, and devising and implementing problem resolution strategies consistent with family cultural values and beliefs (Celano & Kaslow, 2000; Kelly, 2017). Cultural competence also encompasses an attitude of cultural humility, defined as a lifelong process of self-reflection, self-critique, and assessment of power imbalances in relationships (Gallardo, 2014), marked by openness, curiosity, and genuine desire to understand clients' cultural identities and practices.

During treatment planning, the clinician and parents ideally select an intervention demonstrated to be effective with culturally similar families, or an *adaptive* intervention that customizes treatment to a particular family based on assessment of specific cultural tailoring variables (Bernal and Domenech Rodriguez, 2012). In many cases, however, the cultural influences that affect family functioning are not apparent until treatment is underway. In the case of the Medina family, a discussion of cultural beliefs occurred in the fourth session.

The clinician asked Karen to elaborate her statement that she felt "blamed" by Emilio's family for Elena's problems. Karen said Emilio's mother often called to "get a report" on Elena and give parenting advice, which made Karen feel "incompetent." Emilio rose to his mother's defense, claiming she was "just trying to help." The clinician asked Emilio: "What is the most important thing for me to understand about what it means to be Puerto Rican in your family: what are the roles of mothers, fathers, and grandparents?" Emilio explained that mothers were primarily responsible for childcare and running the home, while fathers worked outside the home and took care of family finances. Grandparents were like "second parents": as involved as parents in raising children, if not more so. The clinician then turned to Karen, asking her about the roles of mothers, fathers, and grandparents in her family's cultural tradition. Karen said: "We don't really have a culture, but both my parents were involved in childrearing. In fact, I got better mothering from my father than from my mother." She went on to say that the grandparents' role was to enjoy the grandchildren, but not to discipline them, as that was the parents' job. The clinician said she could now understand how Karen might perceive her mother-in-law as meddling, given that her family's and Emilio's family's culturally influenced beliefs about grandparent roles were so different. Karen acknowledged that understanding the cultural roots of her mother-in-law's behavior was helpful, but did not make it any easier to bear her "interference" in their lives: "if I avoid her calls, she thinks I'm mad at her, and if I tell her what's going on, she gives me advice I don't want to hear." The clinician asked both parents to consider how Karen can preserve her privacy while maintaining a good relationship with her mother-in-law. Emilio suggested that Karen tell his mother that "everything is under control," give her a few details, and then change the subject. "It usually works for me," he said, smiling.

*The clinician praised the couple for working together to understand each other's cultural perspective, and said she had a more difficult question for them. "To what extent do these cultural beliefs **help** or **constrain** you in*

*solving the problems of Elena's anxiety and difficult behavior?" Karen imme-
diately said that her parents' sharing of childrearing tasks with one another
was "a godsend," as her mother "wasn't always up to the task of parenting,
particularly when I was a teenager." She denied that her family's views of the
roles of parents or grandparents constrained her parenting in any way. The
clinician gently challenged this assertion, asking her to imagine what it would
be like for her right now to obtain emotional support and practical advice
without judgment from her father. Had he not accumulated some wisdom
about raising children? Karen agreed that he had, but she had not wanted to
bother him. Emilio pointed out that her father would not be bothered: "he
would do anything for you." When the clinician asked Emilio how his family's
beliefs about parental roles help or constrain his problem-solving efforts, he
hesitated, but then said he might have a stronger relationship with Elena if
he was more involved in her life. Karen reassured him: "you're very involved
in her life—she likes you better than she likes me!" The clinician posed the
question again, asking about the priority of the parent–child relationship versus other relationships in his family's cultural tradition. A guilty look flashed
across Emilio's face as he shared the view that the parent–child relationship is
primary, and important throughout life. He glanced at Karen as he said that
he may have neglected his marriage to focus on the kids.*

In this session, the clinician used a cultural lens to help Karen understand Emilio's mother's *meddling* as culturally influenced, role-congruent
behavior, and elicited Emilio's support in maintaining a measure of privacy for the couple in making parenting decisions, thus building cohesion
in the couple relationship. In addition, the clinician explored potential
strengths (e.g., support from Karen's father) and limitations (Emilio's prioritization of children over marriage) conferred in part by each partner's
family history within a given cultural context.

Ethical and Legal Competency

All clinicians are expected to abide by local laws and the ethics codes specific to their professional disciplines. The scope of laws governing clinical
practice and the number of potential ethical challenges are greater when
working with families than with individuals. There are a number of ethical and legal issues unique to the specialty practice of CFP. The ethical

and legal competency for CFP includes: (a) command of ethical and legal knowledge related to CFP, (b) application of an ethical decision-making model and relevant ethical and legal principles, and (c) commitment to ethical development and improvement in the competency (Stanton & Welsh, 2011).

Like other clinicians, CFP specialists review the limits of confidentiality with family members at the outset of treatment, and obtain informed consent to share specific clinical material with other providers or with school staff. However, confidentiality is more complicated in systemic practice because the definition of the client varies, depending on the case. Prior to entering into a therapeutic alliance, the CFP practitioner must have a clear idea of whether the client is the entire family, a specific dyad (e.g., the couple, or the parent–child relationship), or one (or more) of its constituent members. The definition of the client is dependent on the referred child's presenting problems, the systemic case conceptualization, and the goals of therapy. Adapting Baucom and colleagues' (2012) classification of therapy for couples, there are three types of interventions for families in which a child has a psychiatric disorder: (a) parent-assisted interventions, in which the parent is an agent of change to help the child, as in many CBT interventions; (b) disorder-specific interventions (e.g., PCIT) that target specific relational patterns directly related to the child's disorder; and (c) family therapy, which broadly targets relational difficulties. In only the latter category is the client defined as the family. Even if the family is defined as the client, the medical record may be in the name of the child presenting with the most symptoms.

At the outset of treatment, the clinician should negotiate with the family who will be the client in terms of record-keeping as well as case conceptualization, and which case material is confidential from whom. Clinicians proactively discuss confidentiality (and its limits) with parents and the referred child, as well as the clinician's duty to share clinical impressions about the child with the parents. For the Medina family, the client in terms of case conceptualization and record-keeping is Elena; therapy seeks to change family relationship patterns as a means of reducing Elena's anxiety and oppositional behavior. Using a consent form, the clinician negotiated with the family to share information about Elena's diagnosis, treatment plan, and progress with the pediatrician and relevant school staff. Elena's comments during individual sessions were kept confidential until and unless she gave permission for the clinician to share them with her parents; however, the clinician's interventions and perceptions of her progress in mastering coping skills were routinely shared with the parents.

Should the Clinician Meet Separately with Individuals in the Family?

Many clinicians confront the question of whether they should meet separately with individual family members other than the referred child during systemic treatment. In general, clinicians should see a family member for an individual session only if this decision is consistent with the treatment plan, and unlikely to threaten the systemic therapeutic alliance. Thus, an individual session with the referred child or with a parent is usually acceptable, whereas a session with a sibling typically is not. Sometimes it is necessary to hold an individual session with one family member (e.g., emergency evaluation of a sibling) even if doing so is inconsistent with the treatment plan or may adversely affect the systemic alliance. In this case, the clinician should discuss the pros and cons of doing so with the parents, including the potential impact on confidentiality, the systemic alliance and case conceptualization, preferably before meeting with the individual member.

Even with a treatment plan in place that stipulates who should attend which sessions, many clinicians encounter a situation in which unexpected family members present for an appointment, or fewer family members appear than expected. For example, a child and one parent may attend a session intended for both parents. In that case, the clinician has several options: (a) use the session for an individual child intervention; (b) continue with the planned parents-only intervention, conferencing in the absent parent by phone; (c) reschedule the session for a time when both parents can be present; or (d) meet with the family members present, informing them that the material discussed will be shared with the absent parent, and avoid discussing the absent parent during the session.

According to the treatment plan for the Medina family, individual child sessions included brief updates from Karen on Elena's school attendance and behavior in Elena's presence. Interventions focused on parenting were to be held with both parents together. However, Karen once requested to speak alone with the clinician as a part of Elena's session:

Karen informed the clinician that she and Emilio had been working together satisfactorily to implement the recommended disciplinary strategies until the past week, when Emilio was out of town on business a few nights. When he returned, Elena refused to go to bed on time, and Emilio reportedly "blew up," screaming at his daughter, and threatening dire consequences never discussed in advance (i.e., taking away her birthday party). Karen expressed frustration and anger in the session, and wondered whether Emilio was truly committed to Elena's therapy. She said that she might have to attend future appointments without him. The clinician empathized with how hard it must have been to witness Emilio "blowing up" at Elena, and asked Karen if she had discussed her concerns with Emilio. She said she had not, as she did not know how to approach the topic without upsetting him. The clinician offered to help the two of them discuss the incident in a way that did not embarrass or upset either of them, and could get them back on track, working together as a team to help Elena. She added that further discussion of this topic without Emilio present risked making Emilio feel "unfairly left out" and could contribute to Karen's distorted but familiar belief that she had to do everything by herself, without support.

How Should the Clinician Treat Information Disclosed in an Individual Session?

During the informed consent process, the clinician should establish guidelines for the appropriate use of individual sessions or phone calls, and discuss how information obtained during individual sessions will be handled. An ethical dilemma occurs when a family member discloses secrets to the clinician, such as when a child shares that her parents had a fight, or when a mother confides that she has had an extramarital affair. In the field of CFP, the options for managing this information are: (a) treat all disclosed information as confidential, (b) consider no information as confidential, (c) keep only certain sensitive information confidential, or (d) keep it confidential only temporarily (Snyder & Doss, 2005).

CFP practitioners should not keep secrets, as doing so colludes with one family member against another, jeopardizing the systemic alliance and treatment efficacy. Instead, the clinician should explore why the family member decided to disclose the secret in the session, and develop a plan to share the information with the other relevant family members. For example, a mother who discloses an extramarital affair should be encouraged to share this information with her husband, and the affair should be discussed in the next session for the parents. Children who overhear a parental fight should be supported in discussing their associated feelings and attributions with the parents in the clinician's presence. At times, the clinician's role is to prepare the child to share the secret (e.g., "I might be gay") or question (e.g., "am I adopted?"), while separately coaching the parents to respond optimally, prior to bringing parents and child together to discuss the issue in session.

Some secrets must be kept temporarily to protect the child. In some cases of child abuse or neglect, the clinician may report the maltreatment to the local statutory child protection agency without informing the parent, to protect the child from reprisals. Whether or not the clinician informs the parent about this statutory obligation, the systemic therapeutic alliance can be threatened, and the parent may withdraw the family from treatment. However, child safety should always be prioritized over the therapeutic alliance because children are vulnerable to harm, and there are laws mandating clinicians as reporters of child maltreatment. To report maltreatment in a manner most likely to preserve the systemic alliance, the clinician should: (a) make the report in the parents' presence, (b) disclose only the information needed by the statutory child protection agency to investigate the case, and (c) include information about the family's strengths and participation in treatment. It is often helpful, though difficult, to explore parents' and the clinician's feelings about the decision to report the maltreatment, as well as the impact of the report on the therapeutic alliance.

Should the Same Clinician Treat Two Children from the Same Family?

It is not uncommon for parents to request that the clinician treat a second child in the family, as they already feel comfortable with the clinician and may not want to spend the time and money to *repeat the story* with a new clinician. If the second child's presenting problems can be explained by the existing case conceptualization, the second child can be treated by the same clinician, if doing so is acceptable to the family and does not threaten the systemic alliance. However, an assessment is needed to determine the extent to which the second child's symptoms are due primarily to existing family dynamics, to individual biological or psychological factors, or to other contextual factors. Consider the case of three children ages four to seven years presenting with sibling conflict and oppositional behavior resulting from the parents' poor co-parenting relationship, lack of consistent discipline, and insufficient individual positive attention to the children. All three children would benefit from the same family therapy and parenting interventions; thus, all three could be assigned to the same clinician.

If the second referred child's presenting problems are due in part to individual or contextual factors not addressed in the first referred child's systemic treatment, it is usually best for the second child to be assigned to a different clinician. The second clinician can target the individual and peer or school influences relevant to this child's problems, but the child should continue in the family therapy with the first clinician. This arrangement works best when the two clinicians share information about the family or serve as co-therapists for the family sessions. In communities or service settings in which there is no other qualified clinician available, the existing clinician can evaluate and treat the second child, provided that all family members are aware of the advantages and disadvantages of this arrangement, and give their consent.

Terminating Treatment

The decision to end treatment can be made by the parents, by the clinician, by mutual agreement of both, or by the indirect intervention of a third-party payer. Termination may range from carefully planned to totally unplanned, and the treatment completed (or interrupted) may range from completely successful to unsuccessful. What complicates termination in systemic practice is that there may be differences in opinion among family members about whether and when to end treatment; some may perceive more progress in attaining goals, or experience more treatment burden, than others. Parents have more decision-making power than children, so it is often their decision to end treatment even if the child wants to continue.

A pattern of missed appointments may represent a family's passive attempt to end treatment. If the family misses multiple appointments, the clinician should re-assess their commitment to treatment and their view of how treatment is progressing (see Chapter 5). If the family is ambivalent about continuing, the clinician's strategy will depend in part on the extent to which treatment goals have been attained. If the presenting problems have not been resolved and a sufficient dose of family therapy has not yet been tried, the clinician should try to build the systemic alliance and re-engage the family in the treatment process, rather than actively or passively terminate the therapy. If the family has accomplished some of their treatment goals, the clinician may discuss with them the advantages and disadvantages of continuing versus ending treatment, and arrive at a mutual decision to: (a) continue sessions, possibly at a reduced frequency, (b) end treatment, or (c) take a *break* in treatment for a specified period. When the decision is to terminate treatment, the ending is rarely final. Most clinicians present themselves as available in the future to help solve problems that emerge as children develop and the family faces unanticipated stressors and expected lifecycle changes.

As in all clinical work, a planned termination is preferred over an unplanned ending. The termination trajectory usually bears some proportion to the length of treatment; longer-term family therapy may require a longer termination phase than a brief course of therapy. The tasks of termination include: (a) tracking of client and family progress toward goals to determine when to end treatment, (b) reviewing the course of treatment to build closure and enhance changes that have occurred, (c) highlighting treatment gains and the family's role in these gains, (d) discussing what skills have been learned and how they might be applied later or in other situations, (e) helping the family internalize the clinician (i.e., "what would Dr. X want us to do in this situation?"), (f) saying goodbye, with an opportunity for family members and clinician to express gratitude and exchange feelings, and (g) discussing guidelines for making decisions about returning to treatment (Lebow, 2014). As termination cannot always be carefully planned and is sometimes beyond the family's

or clinician's control, consideration of the tasks of termination throughout treatment is advised. For example, the clinician can draw attention to
the parents' successful management of a new negative child behavior, or
to family members' attempts to repair relationship damage. The goal in
systemic practice is to build relationships and skills within the family, not
dependency on the clinician or the therapy.

*After 12 sessions, Karen and Emilio informed the clinician that it would
be difficult for Elena to attend sessions because they would conflict with her
gymnastics practice. By this point, Elena was attending school consistently,
though she was continuing to test parental limits and show negative behavior (mostly disrespectful tone or screaming) one to two days per week. The
clinician reviewed the family's progress with the parents and again with the
entire family. In the parent session, Karen reported that she and her husband
had confronted a new challenge from Elena the previous weekend: Elena had
thrown a tantrum at a store because her mother refused to buy her a toy. Karen
had been furious and embarrassed, but she had remained calm, even though
Elena continued screaming as they walked to the car. Before leaving the park-
ing lot, she texted Emilio, and together they decided that Karen should give
Elena one warning that if she continued screaming, she would lose her tablet
for the rest of the day, and she would not go out to get ice cream that evening
as they had planned. Karen gave the warning, Elena continued to scream,
and Karen took away her tablet privileges. As Karen had pulled "Elena duty"
all afternoon, Emilio agreed to stay home with Elena while Karen and Julian
went out to get ice cream that evening. The clinician praised the couple for
staying calm, working together, and enforcing the threatened consequences for
a negative behavior displayed in a new setting. She asked them if they wanted
to reduce the frequency of sessions or stop altogether now that they were feeling
more confident and having more success in managing Elena's behavior. After
some discussion, the parents decided to take a "break" from therapy until after
the gymnastics season, but agreed to return earlier if Elena began missing
school or her negative behavior increased.*

Parenting and management of child anxiety are long-term processes
that demand an evolving, expanding repertoire of skills, knowledge, and
attitudes as children develop and face new challenges. It is not possible
to learn, much less remember, every tool or coping skill for every contingency that family members will experience over the lifecycle. Ideally, they

will remember therapy as an investment in positive family relationships, such that they can return to systemic treatment in the future when they need better understanding of one another.

Reflective Practice

To be effective in systemic practice, clinicians must connect deeply and meaningfully with the family while also preserving a strong sense of self. A sense of self refers to one's awareness of one's own values, beliefs, strengths, and vulnerabilities, with relative consistency of these qualities over time and situations. It is natural for clinicians to have strong values about family life, as well as sensitivities to certain family interactions or problems. For example, some clinicians may feel more uncomfortable with family conflict or authoritarian parenting than others. Some may be vulnerable to siding with parents over children or vice versa. Those who have experienced a personal loss should consider how their own bereavement may affect their ability to help a grieving family.

Clinicians do not have to give up their beliefs or overcome all vulnerabilities to help children and families. However, they must be aware of them and their potential impact on their clinical work, consistent with the competency of reflective practice as it is applied to CFP. Reflective practice involves a number of capacities, including openness, self-observation, self-awareness, self-reflection, metacognition, and emotional awareness (Falender, Shafranske, & Falicov, 2014). It is typically described as an internal evaluation process, with the aims of preventing compassion fatigue and competence problems, developing awareness of how one is shaped by ICD factors, and attending to one's health behaviors and well-being, and their impact on specialty practice.

Clinicians who preserve a strong sense of self are not emotionally detached from clients or unchanged by their relationships with families. In fact, if we are truly emotionally available to clients, we run the risk of connecting to their painful experiences in a way that triggers our own painful affect or memories. However, these risks are also opportunities for personal, emotional, and relational growth. Effective family therapy can become a transformational process for clinicians as well as clients. Systemic practice with children and families can yield important lessons about families, human development, and life.

Conclusion

Children's emotional and behavioral disorders are best understood and treated with a CFP approach. This systemic approach is defined by a set of core competencies that serve as the basis for clinical practice. This book has described the competencies most relevant to systemic clinical practice with children and families: scientific knowledge, assessment, evidence-based practice, intervention, individual and cultural diversity, ethical and legal standards, and reflective practice. For information and discussion about all the CFP competencies, readers are referred to Stanton and Welsh (2011) and Celano (in press).

Systemic practice with children and their families requires integration on many levels. First, the clinician must incorporate information from various informants across several domains of functioning to develop a systemic case formulation. Second, individual and dyadic evidence-based practices (e.g., CBT, cohesion-building strategies) are integrated into a set of interventions guided by a systemic case formulation. Third, clinicians integrate specific practice methods to match their comfort level, preferences, and interpersonal interaction skills. Some intervention strategies are a more natural fit for one clinician than another, and many clinicians adopt and utilize new methods of practice over time. As a result, systemic treatment offered by one clinician may look different than that offered by another. However, systemic intervention is most effective when therapists shape their own methods of practice (Lebow, 2014).

Systemic therapy is among the most complex of psychological and psychotherapeutic practices, requiring clinicians to simultaneously negotiate complicated relational systems, understand the perspective of each family member without sacrificing the systemic alliance, tailor interventions to individual and cultural diversity factors, track family interactions, and monitor treatment progress. In addition, clinicians need to learn multiple interventions, as one intervention does not work for all families or in all situations. Given the complexity of systemic practice, competency-based training and supervision by experts in CFP is essential.

Finally, systemic practice is client-centered. The expressed goals and needs of children, parents, and families are what drive treatment. Clinicians must keep in mind how the therapy appears or is experienced by clients (Lebow, 2014), regardless of the evidence base for the intervention.

Given the increasing cultural diversity and change in predominant family forms (e.g., increase in single-parent families) in the United States (Pew Research Center, 2015), a client-centered approach ensures that systemic practice is beneficial and relevant to children, families, and communities.

References

American Psychological Association. (2017). *Multicultural guidelines: An ecological approach to context, identity, and intersectionality.* Washington, DC: Author.

Bernal, G., & Domenech Rodriguez, M. M. (2012). *Cultural adaptations: Tools for evidence-based practice with diverse populations.* Washington, DC: American Psychological Association.

Baucom, D. H., Whisman, M. A., & Paprocki, C. (2012). Couple-based interventions for psychopathology. *Journal of Family Therapy, 34*(3), 250–270.

Celano, M. P., & Kaslow, N. J. (2000). Culturally competent family interventions: Review and case illustrations. *American Journal of Family Therapy, 28*(3), 217–228.

Falender, C. A., Shafranske, E. P., & Falicov, C. (2014). Reflective practice: Culture in self and other. In C. A. Falender, E. P. Shafranske, & C. Falicov (Eds.), *Multiculturalism and diversity in clinical supervision: A competency-based approach* (pp. 273–281). Washington, DC: American Psychological Association.

Gallardo, M. E. (2014). *Developing cultural humility: Embracing race, privilege and power.* Thousand Oaks, CA: Sage Publications.

Kelly, S. (2017). Conclusions drawn from the experts on tailoring treatment to diverse couples and families. In S. Kelly (Ed.), *Diversity in couple and family therapy: Ethnicities, sexualities, and socioeconomics* (pp. 453–467). Santa Barbara, CA: Praeger/ABC-CLIO.

Lebow, J. (2014). *Couple and family therapy: An integrative map of the territory.* Washington, DC: American Psychological Association.

Pew Research Center. (2015). *Parenting in America: Outlook, worries, aspirations are strongly linked to financial situation.* Retrieved November 11, 2017, from http://pewsocialtrends.org/2015/12/17/1-the-american-family-today/

Snyder, D. K., & Doss, B. D. (2005). Treating infidelity: Clinical and ethical directions. *Journal of Clinical Psychology, 61*(11), 1453–1465.

Stanton, M., & Welsh, R. (2011). *Specialty competencies in couple and family psychology.* Oxford: Oxford University Press.

About the Author

Marianne Celano, PhD, ABPP is a Professor in the Department of Psychiatry and Behavioral Sciences of Emory University School of Medicine. A board certified Couple and Family Psychologist, she specializes in treatment of children with emotional and behavioral problems. She is certified in both Trauma-Focused Cognitive Behavioral Therapy (TF-CBT) and Parent–Child Interaction Therapy (PCIT). At Emory, she directs family therapy training for child psychiatry residents, and she has been active in teaching psychology interns, postdoctoral fellows, and residents for over 25 years. Her scholarly work focuses on family therapy training, behavioral health services for maltreated children, and the development and evaluation of family interventions.

Index

ABPP. *See* American Board of
    Professional Psychology
American Academy of Child and
    Adolescent Psychiatry, 8
American Board of Professional
    Psychology (ABPP), 5
Anxiety disorders, 46–48

Behavioral health assessment, 30
Behavioral health organizations, 2
Biological and psychological child
    factors, 14–15

Case formulation
    role in selection of interventions,
        52–53
    systemic case conceptualization, 6,
        40–43
CFP. *See* Couple and family
    psychology
Child behavioral and emotional
    problems, 5
Child behavior problems, 13–14
Child development
    developmental considerations in
        treatment, 65–66, 69, 81
    developmental models, 7
    developmentally appropriate
        interventions, 55–56
    psychopathology, 13, 25
    role in assessment, 30, 36–37,
        41, 43
Child Effects on Parent and Family
    Processes, 15–16
Client-centered perspective, 35–37
Clinical interview, 30–32
Clinical rating scales, 33
Coding schemes, 33
Cohesion, 68–70
Collaborative treatment planning,
    57–60

Competencies
    assessment, 29–43
    benchmarks for application
        domain, 10
    ethical and legal, 88–93
    individual and cultural diversity,
        85–88
    intervention, 65–81
    reflective practice, 96
Couple and family psychology (CFP)
    competency benchmarks, 10
    Definition, 5–6
    treatment of children, 7–9
Couple and family psychology (CFP)
        assessment methods
    client-centered perspectives, 35–37
    clinical interview, 30–32
    observational methods, 33–35
    self-report instruments, 32–33
Couple distress, 51–52

Depression, parental, 19
Disparities in behavioral health care,
    21–22
Disruptive behavior, 14, 49–51

Economic hardship, 21
Ethical competency, 88–93
Evidence-based interventions
    anxiety disorders, 46–48
    case formulation, 52–53
    couple distress, 51–52
    criteria for selection of
        interventions, 53–54
    developmentally appropriate,
        55–56
    disruptive behavior, 49–51
    durability, 55
    efficacy, 54
    efficiency, 55
    school refusal, 48–49

Family systems orientation
  relationship to family therapy,
    to CFP, 9
  role in clinical decisions, 2–5
Family causal factors, 16
Family functioning and child
    psychopathology
  biological and psychological child
    factors, 14–15
  child effects on parent and family
    processes, 15–16
  family causal factors, 16
  interparental conflict, 18
  parental depression, 19
  parenting, 16–18
  system-wide family dynamics,
    19–20
  temperament, 15
Family organization, 72–74
See Couple and Family Psychology
  (CFP)

Help-seeking, 21–22

Individual and cultural diversity
    (ICD) competency, 85–88
Interdisciplinary collaboration,
    76–77
Interparental conflict, 18

Legal competency, 88–93

Neighborhood context, 20–21

Observational methods, 33–35

Parental depression, 19
Parenting
  assessment, 29
  co-parenting, 19

effect of economic hardship, 21
interventions, 49–51, 72–74
role in child psychopathology 7,
  16–18, 25
Problem formulation, 41
Psychoeducation, 75
Psychological child factors, 14–15

Reflective practice, 96

School refusal, 48–49
Self-report instruments, 32–33
Systemic case conceptualization
  case formulation, 41–43
  definition, 40–41
  problem formulation, 41
Systemic interventions
  building cohesion, 68–70
  interdisciplinary collaboration,
    76–77
  monitoring treatment progress,
    77–81
  managing negative interactions,
    70–72
  parenting/family organization,
    72–74
  psychoeducation, 75
  systemic therapeutic alliance,
    66–68
Systemic therapeutic alliance
  alliance repair, 79
  definition, 66
  forging a systemic alliance, 66–68
  split alliance, 78
Systems of care, 7–8, 23–25
System-wide family dynamics,
  19–20

Temperament, 15
Terminating treatment, 93–96

TITLES FROM OUR PSYCHOLOGY COLLECTION

Anthony Chambers and Corinne Datchi, Editors

Justice in Life and Society: How We Decide What is Fair
by Virginia Murphy-Berman

A Guide for Statistics in the Behavioral Sciences
by Jeff Foster

*College Student Psychological Adjustment: Exploring Relational
Dynamics that Predict Success*
by Jonathan F. Mattanah

*College Student Psychological Adjustment:
Theory, Methods, and Statistical Trends*
by Jonathan F. Mattanah

Perfectionism in School: When Achievement Is Not so Perfect
by Kathryn L. Fletcher and Kristie L. Speirs Neumeister

Momentum Press is one of the leading book publishers in the field of engineering, mathematics, health, and applied sciences. Momentum Press offers over 30 collections, including Aerospace, Biomedical, Civil, Environmental, Nanomaterials, Geotechnical, and many others.

Momentum Press is actively seeking collection editors as well as authors. For more information about becoming an MP author or collection editor, please visit http://www.momentumpress.net/contact

Announcing Digital Content Crafted by Librarians

Momentum Press offers digital content as authoritative treatments of advanced engineering topics by leaders in their field. Hosted on ebrary, MP provides practitioners, researchers, faculty, and students in engineering, science, and industry with innovative electronic content in sensors and controls engineering, advanced energy engineering, manufacturing, and materials science.

Momentum Press offers library-friendly terms:

- perpetual access for a one-time fee
- no subscriptions or access fees required
- unlimited concurrent usage permitted
- downloadable PDFs provided
- free MARC records included
- free trials

The **Momentum Press** digital library is very affordable, with no obligation to buy in future years.

For more information, please visit **www.momentumpress.net/library** or to set up a trial in the US, please contact **mpsales@globalepress.com**.

www.ingramcontent.com/pod-product-compliance
Lightning Source LLC
Chambersburg PA
CBHW052016230326
41598CB00078B/3508

* 9 7 8 1 9 4 5 6 1 2 9 8 5 *